FIFTY-FIFTY

BOOK TWO
AN INTERMEDIATE COURSE
IN COMMUNICATIVE ENGLISH

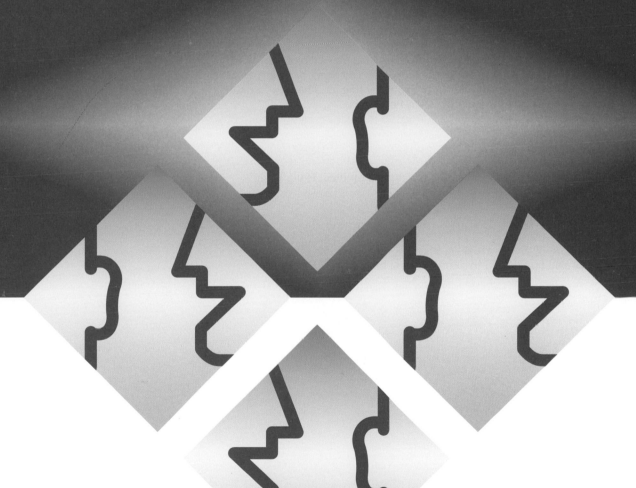

Warren Wilson   Roger Barnard

SECOND EDITION

Longman

Published by
Longman Asia ELT
2/F Cornwall House
Taikoo Place
979 King's Road
Quarry Bay
Hong Kong

fax: +852 2856 9578
e-mail: aelt@pearsoned.com.hk
website: www.longman-elt.com

and Associated Companies throughout the world.

First published 1998
Reprinted 2001 (twice)

Produced by Pearson Education North Asia Limited, Hong Kong
GCC/03

ISBN 0 13 920034 7

Illustrated by Andrew Lange, Megan Cash and Roger Barnard
Cover and text design by Siren Design, Inc.

Contents ────────────────────────────────

Acknowledgments

We would like to thank the teachers and students at the following schools for their valuable help in developing and revising this material:

Athénée-Français, Tokyo
Community English Program, Teachers College, Columbia University, New York
Cosmopolitan Language Institute, Tokyo
English Language Institute, Queens College, New York
International English Language Institute, Hunter College, New York
Tama Art University, Tokyo
Tokyo School of Business, Tokyo

We would also like to thank those at Prentice Hall who worked on this project originally, particularly our editor, Nancy Baxer and production editor, Noël Vreeland Carter. For this new edition, we thank our editor, Nancy Baxer once again, and the great people at Prentice Hall Asia ELT, as well as the talented people at Siren design, Inc., particularly Matthew Zuch and Nancy Sharkey. And a special thanks to Andrew Lange and Megan Montegue Cash for their great artwork, and Rich LePage for his expert recording work.

For In Sook, Masako, Mia, and Sophie.

R.B.
W.W.
Tokyo/New York
September 1998

Introduction

Fifty-Fifty is a three-level course in communicative English that provides listening and speaking practice for students from the low elementary level through the intermediate level. Designed primarily for use in large classes where "student-talking" time is usually very limited, this material can be used effectively in virtually any size class since students actively participate in meaningful exchanges during pair work and group work. The focus is on listening and speaking proficiency. *Fifty-Fifty* provides realistic yet doable listening tasks and solid pair work and group work tasks, all of which are designed to reduce learner anxiety and promote language acquisition via student participation in purposeful interaction and extended discourse.

Fifty-Fifty Book Two has been designed as a follow-up course to *Fifty-Fifty Book One: A Basic Course in Communicative English,* but it can be used independently in classes at the intermediate level. The text consists of a warm-up unit, twelve main units, and three review units. Every fifth unit consolidates and recycles the material covered in the preceding units. The appendix contains the *Student B* pages of the pair work activities and a *Homework* assignment for each unit, as well as the tapescript for the listening tasks and *Grammar Summaries* for the main units.

Each unit provides the students with a brief presentation of the language point to be practiced, a listening task centered around the language point, and extensive oral/aural practice in which the students use the language to complete specific tasks. The *Homework* section of each main unit provides written practice in the material covered, thus reinforcing spelling and vocabulary as well as further demonstrating the language in context.

Each unit consists of the following sections. (The format of the review units differs slightly.)

WARM-UP EXERCISES

Each unit begins with a simple warm-up exercise in the form of a comic sketch. The sketch has one empty speech balloon to be filled in by the student. The sketch illustrates the unit theme and introduces, in a simple context, the language to be practiced.

Exercise 2 and Exercise 3 center on a dialog that functions as a model that the students can listen to and practice reading through with a partner. Once the students are familiar with its language and content, they can practice the dialog using substitutions that are provided. The dialog can also be used for freer conversation practice in which the students supply their own information.

LISTENING TASK

The *Listening Task* helps the students focus on the particular language points to be practiced. The students are not expected to retain or reproduce *all* the language they hear on the tape, but their aural comprehension of the target structures and vocabulary will increase as they listen for the information needed to complete the task.

It is suggested that the teacher play the tape several times: once to familiarize the students with the content, then again with pauses as the students complete the task, and once more straight through as they check their answers. After the teacher has elicited the answers, the students could listen a final time, perhaps while going over the tapescript. The tapescript for the *Listening Task* is located in the appendix and can also be used for extended practice and/or review of grammar and vocabulary. The *Teacher's Edition* provides helpful hints, as well as the answers, to ensure that the exercise goes smoothly.

PAIR WORK

The *Pair Work* section provides communicative practice that maximizes "student-talking" time. Students complete the task by asking partners for missing information. Being task-based, the exercise provides more than just question-and-answer practice: genuine communication takes place. The completion of each task relies on actual information sharing and feedback between students conversing in pairs.

It is suggested that the teacher try having students sit face to face, if possible, and maintain eye contact while speaking. They should avoid looking at each other's pages and should always ask for spelling or repetition in English. It is advisable to circulate once quickly at the outset to make sure that each student understands what to do and gets off to a good start. Correction techniques vary from teacher to teacher and exercise to exercise; however, during communicative practice it is usually advisable to leave most correction until afterwards. The point of the tasks is communication, not the production of flawless sentences. (Nevertheless, errors that interfere with comprehension and/or are counterproductive to the practice should be rectified appropriately.)

Finally, the teacher can check the finished work by scanning students' pages and briefly querying their partners to verify answers. Students can also confer and compare answers themselves.

GROUP WORK

The *Group Work* activities, by their very nature, involve more class interaction than the *Pair Work* activities, and usually demand more spontaneous communication because of the faster pace and frequent changing of partners. *Group Work* exercises include "find someone who" activities, group interviews, and various types of language games that promote interaction while lessening learner anxiety.

All suggestions given above for the *Pair Work* section apply to this section; the recommended procedures are the same.

Language Game

In the review units, *Group Work* is followed by a section labeled *Language Game,* an activity that encourages focused listening. The point of the game is to provide ample comprehensible input containing vocabulary and structures from the preceding units, as well as pronunciation practice —hopefully more in an atmosphere of fun, and less of conscious language study.

HOMEWORK

The appendix contains the *Homework* section, which provides one homework assignment for each main unit. The teacher might prefer to have students do the assignment on a separate sheet of paper to be handed in.

Some *Homework* pages provide an optional follow-up exercise for in-class use, time permitting.

Please note that some of these optional exercises might require the teacher's review of the students' homework beforehand.

STUDENT B PAGES

This section in the appendix contains all the pages necessary for the information gap activities, when students working in pairs or small groups must look at different pages. In the units, these activities contain a page reference box in the upper right hand corner:

STUDENT B:
LOOK AT
PAGE 78

TAPESCRIPT

The tapescript in the appendix contains all the listening material presented on the accompanying audio cassette—except for the introductory dialog in the *Warm-up Exercises* of each unit (since the dialog itself serves as the tapescript).

GRAMMAR SUMMARIES

The *Grammar Summaries* section in the appendix contains an overview of the sentence structures presented in each of the twelve main units, providing language models for the students.

The Teacher's Edition

The *Teacher's Edition* provides additional suggestions and helpful hints for each activity as well as the answers for the listening exercises. It is meant to be used as a tool to aid in lesson preparation and in-class use of the material—*not* as a set of guidelines or instructions to be followed.

The authors hope you and your students enjoy using *Fifty-Fifty* and would appreciate any comments or suggestions you might have.

GETTING STARTED

WARM-UP EXERCISES

EXERCISE 1

Write one or two sentences in the empty speech balloon.

EXERCISE 2

Practice the following conversation with a partner. (Take turns as *Paul* and *Jane*.)

Paul:	Hello. I'm Paul Savage.
Jane:	Nice to meet you. My name's Jane... Jane Chung.
Paul:	Glad to meet you, Jane. Where are you from?
Jane:	Well, I'm from San Francisco, but I live in New Jersey now. So, what do you do, Paul?
Paul:	I'm studying law here at Columbia. How about you?
Jane:	I'm a software designer. I work for Nintendo.
Paul:	Oh, really? So why are you studying Japanese?
Jane:	I'm going to work in our Tokyo office next year.

EXERCISE 3

Practice the conversation a few more times, with a different partner each time. This time, use true information about yourself (or make up your own information).

> **Memo**
> • ALWAYS LOOK AT THE PERSON YOU ARE SPEAKING TO— DON'T LOOK DOWN AT THE TEXT!

LISTENING TASK   *Do Exercise 1 alone and Exercise 2 with a partner.*

EXERCISE 1

Listen to the conversation and check (√) all the correct information for John and Maria.

	is from Denver	is from Chicago	lives in Denver	lives in Chicago	is a teacher	is a graphic designer	plays tennis	goes to art shows
John	☐	☐	☐	☐	☐	☐	☐	☐
Maria	☐	☐	☐	☐	☐	☐	☐	☐

EXERCISE 2

Work with a partner and take turns asking each other "yes/no" questions about John and Maria. (Ask questions with your book open, and answer with your book *closed.*)

Examples:

Student A: *Is Maria from <u>Denver</u>?*
Student B: *No, she isn't.*

Student A: *Does John live in <u>Chicago</u>?*
Student B: *Yes, he does.*

PAIR WORK

Student A

STUDENT B:
LOOK AT
PAGE 78

EXERCISE 1

Take turns with *Student B* asking and answering questions about the three people, and fill in the blanks in the boxes (1 through 3).

Memo
· USE "SHE", "HE",
AND "THEY"
IN YOUR QUESTIONS
AND ANSWERS
(IN BOXES 1-3).

Example:

Student A: Where does Jenny live?
Student B: She lives in Malibu.

1
Jenny
I live in .... and I'm a movie actress. I like to practice yoga and I love to go surfing. I can speak ....

2
Phil
*I'm a .... In my free time I ....
I live in Berlin and I can speak German and French.*

3
Harry and Lisa
*We are both .... and we live in ....
We both can speak Japanese and we love to go hiking and camping.*

4
....
....
....
....
name
Student B

EXERCISE 2

Take turns with *Student B* asking and answering the same questions about each other for box 4. Then write a paragraph about *Student B* in box 4.

Use "you" in your questions, and "he" or "she" in your paragraph.

GROUP WORK   *Do Exercise 1 alone and Exercise 2 with everyone.*

a. • New Orleans
   • Munich
   • Singapore

b. • travel writer
   • artist
   • hotel manager

c. • French
   • German
   • Chinese

d. • horseback riding
   • hang gliding
   • rollerblading

EXERCISE 1

Fill in each blank below with information from the box on the left. (Use this information to answer questions in *Exercise 2*.)

a. *Your residence:* ....
b. *Your occupation:* ....
c. *Your language:* ....
d. *Your hobby:* ....

EXERCISE 2

Walk around the classroom and ask questions. For each sentence (a~d), find someone with the *same* answer as you and write his or her name in the box below.

a. .... name
b. .... name
c. .... name
d. .... name

Example:

Student A: Where do you live?
Student B: I live in Singapore.

1 JUST ASKING

WARM-UP EXERCISES

EXERCISE 1

Write one question in each empty speech balloon.

EXERCISE 2

Practice the following conversation with a partner. (Take turns as the *clerk* and the *customer*.)

Clerk:	Can I help you?
Customer:	Yes, I'd like some information about the trains.
Clerk:	Yes?
Customer:	Could you tell me what time the train to Miami leaves?
Clerk:	Yes, the next train leaves at 11:00 a.m.
Customer:	Do you know how long it takes?
Clerk:	Sure, it takes eighteen hours.
Customer:	Great. Thank you very much.

EXERCISE 3

Practice the conversation a few more times with your partner. Each time, ask and answer questions about the information below.

Memo

- ALWAYS LOOK AT THE PERSON YOU ARE SPEAKING TO—DON'T LOOK DOWN AT THE TEXT!
- YOU CAN ALSO MAKE UP YOUR OWN INFORMATION.

LISTENING TASK

EXERCISE 1

Listen to the conversations (1 through 4) and write
the number of each conversation on the correct picture.

Memo
• YOU ONLY HEAR
ONE SIDE OF EACH
TELEPHONE
CONVERSATION.

EXERCISE 2

Listen to each conversation again. As you listen,
make a note of the questions that each woman asks
next to the conversation.

Memo
• EXERCISE 2
CAN BE DONE
WITH A PARTNER
OR IN A SMALL GROUP.

PAIR WORK

STUDENT B:
LOOK AT
PAGE 79

EXERCISE 1

1. You are going to take a bus trip from New York City to *Miami* or *Denver*.
Choose *which city* you want to go and *when* you want to leave.
Write the information in the blanks below before you speak to *Student B*:

I'd like to go to .... on ....
   city   day
at about .... o'clock in the ....
          time   time of day

2. *Student B* works at the Port Authority Bus Terminal. Ask *Student B* for
information and write the answers on the memo pad on the right.

Example:

Student B: *Can I help you?*
Student A: *Yes, I'd like to go to <u>Miami</u> on <u>Monday</u> at about <u>7</u> o'clock*
in the <u>morning</u>.
Student B: *Okay, we have buses around that time.*
Student A: *Great! Could you tell me . . .?*

NOTES
How Much?
When leave?
When arrive?
How long?

NEW YORK PENN STATION TRAIN INFORMATION				
DESTINATION:	*CHICAGO*		*L.A.*	
FARE:	$135		$247	
	Departs	Arrives	Departs	Arrives
	10:00	5:15	10:00	9:30
DAILY	11:15	6:30	11:15	10:45
DEPARTURE	12:45	8:00	12:45	12:15
AND	14:00	9:15	14:00	13:30
ARRIVAL	15:30	10:45	15:30	15:00
TIMES:	17:15	12:30	17:15	16:45
	19:45	15:00	19:45	19:15
	21:30	16:45	21:30	21:00
ARRIVAL DAY:	*+ one day*		*+ two days*	
TRAVEL TIME:	*18 hrs. 15 min.*		*44 hrs. 30 min.*	

EXERCISE 2

You work at New York Penn Station. Look at the
train informaton and answer *Student B's* questions.

EXERCISE 3

You are the manager of a language school.
Student B wants to take a language course.
Answer *Student B's* questions.
(Make up the answers!)

Example:

Student B: *Could you tell me if you have a Chinese course?*
Student A: *Yes, we do.*
Student B: *Okay, could you tell me . . .?*

Memo
• DO EXERCISE 3
AGAIN—TAKE TURNS
AS <u>STUDENT A</u> AND
<u>STUDENT B</u>.

GROUP WORK   *Do this exercise with everyone.*

The teacher will give you *one* of the boxes on page 8 or 9.
Walk around the classroom and ask for information and give information.
Write an answer in each blank in your box.

Example:

Student A: *Do you know how long it takes to go from England to France by ferry?*

Student B: *Yes, it takes one and a half hours.*

1

Find someone who knows this information:

• It takes _____ to go from England to France by ferry.
• It costs _____ to go from England to France by ferry.
• _____ is the best season to visit Greece.

- -

Give this information to anyone who asks for it:

• A train ticket from Tokyo to Osaka for the *bullet train* costs about $125.
• Two places to visit in San Francisco are the Golden Gate Bridge and Fisherman's Wharf.
• It takes about 3½ hours to fly from Australia to New Zealand.

Answer "I don't know" to all other questions.

2

Find someone who knows this information:

• It costs _____ to take a horse-and-buggy ride in Central Park in New York City.
• _____ is the cheapest way to travel from New York to California.
• _____ are good places to go sightseeing in San Francisco.

- -

Give this information to anyone who asks for it:

• It takes about 1½ hours to go from England to France by ferry.
• It takes about 2½ hours to go from Tokyo to Osaka by the *bullet train*.
• It's cold in Australia in July. (It's winter!)

Answer "I don't know" to all other questions.

3

Find someone who knows this information:

• It takes _____ to travel by train from Tokyo to Osaka.
• It costs _____ to travel by train from Tokyo to Osaka.
• Most of the subways stop running in Tokyo at about _____ o'clock.

- -

Give this information to anyone who asks for it:

• Springtime is the best time of the year to visit Greece.
• January is the best month to travel through Australia.
• The cheapest way to travel from New York to California is by bus.

Answer "I don't know" to all other questions.

4

Find someone who knows this information:

• _____ is the best month to travel through Australia.
• In July, the weather in Australia is _____ .
• It takes _____ to fly from Australia to New Zealand.

- -

Give this information to anyone who asks for it:

• A ferry ticket costs about $50 one way from England to France.
• Most of the subways in Tokyo stop running about one o'clock in the morning.
• It costs about $40 to take a horse-and-buggy ride in Central Park in New York City.

Answer "I don't know" to all other questions.

Example:

Student B: *Excuse me, could you tell me the cheapest way to travel from New York to California?*

Student C: *I'm sorry, I don't know.*

5

Find someone who knows this information:

• In August, the weather in India is ....

• In January, the weather in Thailand is ....

• The banks open at .... in the morning in Hong Kong.

- -

Give this information to anyone who asks for it:

• A cup of coffee costs about $3.50 at a sidewalk café in Paris.
• Springtime is the best season to trek in the Himalayas.
• It costs about $350 round trip for a discount flight from New York to London.

Answer "I don't know" to all other questions.

6

Find someone who knows this information:

• It takes .... to fly from New York to London.
• It costs .... to fly from New York to London.
• It costs .... to see a movie in London.

- -

Give this information to anyone who asks for it:

• Most of the shops in Barcelona are closed for *siesta* from 1:30 to 3:30 in the afternoon.
• The best way to travel from Hong Kong to Macau is by *jetfoil*, the fastest ferry.
• It's very hot in Thailand in January.

Answer "I don't know" to all other questions.

7

Find someone who knows this information:

• .... is the best way to travel from Hong Kong to Macau.
• .... are good places to go sightseeing in Beijing, China.
• .... is the best season to trek in the Himalayas.

- -

Give this information to anyone who asks for it:

• The banks in Hong Kong open at nine o'clock in the morning.
• It takes about 7½ hours to fly from New York to London.
• Two places to visit in Athens are the Plaka and the Parthenon.

Answer "I don't know" to all other questions.

8

Find someone who knows this information:

• A cup of coffee costs .... at a sidewalk café in Paris.
• The shops are closed from .... to .... for at *siesta* in Barcelona, Spain.
• .... are good places to go sightseeing in Athens, Greece.

- -

Give this information to anyone who asks for it:

• It's hot and rainy in India in August.

• It costs about $8.00 to see a movie in London.

• Two places to visit in Beijing are the Great Wall and the Forbidden City.

Answer "I don't know" to all other questions.

WARM-UP EXERCISES

EXERCISE 1

Write one or two sentences in the empty speech balloon.

EXERCISE 2

Practice the following conversation with a partner. (Take turns as the *customer* and the *waitress*.)

Customer:	**Excuse me, I left my briefcase under my table, and—**
Waitress:	**When was that?**
Customer:	**This morning—about thirty minutes ago.**
Waitress:	**What does it look like?**
Customer:	**It's brown and it has a black handle.**
Waitress:	**Oh, yes. Does it have a combination lock?**
Customer:	**Yes, it does.**
Waitress:	**Right, the bus boy found it. Wait here, I'll get it.**

EXERCISE 3

Practice the conversation a few more times with your partner. Each time, describe one of the objects below.

VOCABULARY
- *camera bag*
- *shopping bag*
- *umbrella*

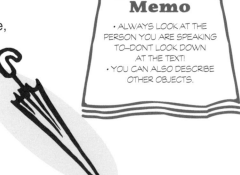

Memo
- ALWAYS LOOK AT THE PERSON YOU ARE SPEAKING TO—DON'T LOOK DOWN AT THE TEXT!
- YOU CAN ALSO DESCRIBE OTHER OBJECTS.

LISTENING TASK

EXERCISE 1

Look at each sentence in the box (*a* through *o*)
and write the letter below each object that it describes.

a. It's made of leather.	**f.** It has a little plastic window.	**k.** It has a strap.
b. It has a handle.	**g.** It's brown.	**l.** There are numbers on it.
c. It's black.	**h.** It's plain, with almost no design.	**m.** It has a lock.
d. It has buttons.	**i.** It has batteries.	**n.** It's made of wood.
e. It's made mostly of plastic.	**j.** It has switches.	**o.** It's square.

EXERCISE 2

Listen to the conversations (1 through 6) and write the
number of each conversation above the correct object.

EXERCISE 3

Listen again and write the *key words* next to each object.

UNIT 2   11

PAIR WORK

Student A:

Choose any eight objects in the picture below.
- Write the numbers 1 through 8 on the objects.
- Then describe each object to *Student B*.

Student B:

Listen to *Student A* describe eight objects.
Write the number on each object (1 through 8).
Ask questions to check!

Memo
- STUDENT A: DON'T SAY WHAT EACH OBJECT IS, OR WHAT IT IS USED FOR.
- DO THIS EXERCISE AGAIN—TAKE TURNS AS STUDENT A AND STUDENT B.

UNIT 2

GROUP WORK

Do this exercise in a group of three or four students.

Student A:

Choose one object in the room below, but don't say which object it is.
Students B, C, and D will ask you questions to find out which object it is.
Answer all questions with "Yes" or "No."

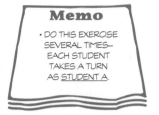

Memo

• DO THIS EXERCISE
SEVERAL TIMES—
EACH STUDENT
TAKES A TURN
AS STUDENT A.

Students B, C, & D:

Take turns asking *Student A* "yes/no" questions. Try to guess *Student A's* object.
Whoever guesses the object first wins. *If no one can guess it,* Student A *wins!*

The group can ask <u>twenty</u> questions—and each student can make <u>three</u> guesses.

"Yes/no" Questions

• *Is it <u>small</u>?*
• *Does it have a <u>handle</u>?*
• *Is it made of <u>plastic</u>?*

WARM-UP EXERCISES

EXERCISE 1

Write one or two sentences in the empty speech balloon.

Do you think you could give me a push?

EXERCISE 2

Practice the following conversation with a partner. (Take turns as *Mom* and *Joey*.)

Mom:	Joey, can I talk to you?
Joey:	Sure, Mom. What is it?
Mom:	Would you mind turning down the volume?
Joey:	Not at all.
Mom:	Could you possibly clean your room this afternoon?
Joey:	Sorry, but I have to go to soccer practice.
Mom:	Well, do you think you could clean it after dinner?
Joey:	Sure, no problem.

Memo
- ALWAYS LOOK AT THE PERSON YOU ARE SPEAKING TO—DON'T LOOK DOWN AT THE TEXT!
- YOU CAN ALSO MAKE UP YOUR OWN REQUESTS.

EXERCISE 3

Practice the conversation a few more times with your partner. Each time, use one of the ideas below to make a request.

VOCABULARY
- *clean the backyard*
- *mow the lawn*
- *take out the garbage*

LISTENING TASK

EXERCISE 1

Listen to the conversation and circle the things that Julie asks Larry to do.

EXERCISE 2

Listen again and check (√) all the things that Larry agrees to do, and make an "X" on the things he can't do.

EXERCISE 3

Listen once more and make a note of *why* he can't do some things.

PAIR WORK

Memo

• FIRST DISCUSS THE POSSIBLE REQUESTS FOR EACH PICTURE.

EXERCISE 1

Make an "X" on six of the things below that you do *not* want to do for your partner, and think of a reason to say "No." (Don't show your partner which six things you have chosen.)

EXERCISE 2

Use different pictures and take turns asking each other to do things.
You must agree to do anything not marked with an "X."

The first person to get his or her partner to say "yes" to six things is the winner!

Memo

• ALWAYS GIVE A REASON WHEN YOU SAY 'NO'.

Example:

Student A: *Do you think you could feed the cat?*
Student B: *Sure, I'd be glad to.*

16   UNIT 3

GROUP WORK   *Do this exercise with everyone.*

The teacher will give you *one* of the boxes on page 17 or 18.
Walk around the classroom and ask other people to do things for you,
and agree—or refuse—to do things for other people.
Write the name of one person who agrees in each blank.

Example:
Student A: *Do you think you could help me look for my dog?*
Student B: *Of course.*

Memo
• ALL OF THE BOXES ON ONE OR BOTH OF THE PAGES MUST BE USED.
• DO NOT SHOW YOUR BOX TO ANYONE!
• TALK TO ONE PERSON AT A TIME.

1

Find someone who:

[name] will drive you to the airport tomorrow evening.

[name] will baby-sit your little brother tonight.

[name] will let you copy yesterday's class notes.

- -

Agree to:

• pick up some books at the library.

• lend your friend ten dollars.

• take care of your friend's cat this summer.

Refuse all other requests!

2

Find someone who:

[name] will lend you ten dollars.

[name] will help you look for your dog.

[name] will water your house plants while you're away next week.

- -

Agree to:

• let your friend copy your class notes.

• help your friend carry some boxes downstairs.

• go to the post office for your friend.

Refuse all other requests!

3

Find someone who:

[name] will help you with the homework after school.

[name] will take care of your cat for a month this summer.

[name] will go to the post office and mail some letters for you.

- -

Agree to:

• teach your friend how to use the computer lab.

• water your friend's house plants.

• baby-sit your friend's little brother.

Refuse all other requests!

4

Find someone who:

[name] will teach you how to use the computer lab after class.

[name] will pick up some books for you at the library this afternoon.

[name] will help you carry some boxes downstairs.

- -

Agree to:

• drive your friend to the airport.

• look for your friend's dog.

• help your friend with the homework.

Refuse all other requests!

Example:

Student B: *Could you possibly help me paint my kitchen this afternoon?*

Student C: *I'm sorry, but I have a dentist appointment.*

5

Find someone who:

_____ (name) will lend you a dictionary.

_____ (name) will pick up your laundry tomorrow morning.

_____ (name) will help you paint your kitchen this afternoon.

- -

Agree to:

• lend your friend a videocamera.

• let your friend copy your homework.

• show your friend how to program a new VCR.

Refuse all other requests!

6

Find someone who:

_____ (name) will let you copy the homework for tomorrow.

_____ (name) will help you move to a new house on Sunday.

_____ (name) will feed your goldfish while you're on vacation next week.

- -

Agree to:

• lend your friend a dictionary.

• go to the bank for your friend.

• go to the supermarket for your friend.

Refuse all other requests!

7

Find someone who:

_____ (name) will help you fix your car.

_____ (name) will show you how to program your new VCR.

_____ (name) will go to the supermarket for you.

- -

Agree to:

• explain the class project to your friend.

• feed your friend's goldfish.

• pick up your friend's laundry.

Refuse all other requests!

8

Find someone who:

_____ (name) will explain the class project to you after school.

_____ (name) will lend you a videocamera for a week.

_____ (name) will go to the bank for you this afternoon.

- -

Agree to:

• help paint your friend's kitchen.

• help your friend move to a new house.

• help fix your friend's car.

Refuse all other requests!

---

4 TURN IT CLOCKWISE

WARM-UP EXERCISES

EXERCISE 1

Write a question in the second speech balloon.

EXERCISE 2

Practice the following conversation with a partner. (Take turns as the *man* and the *woman*.)

Man:	Excuse me, could you tell me how to buy a ticket?
Woman:	Sure. First, find the price of your station on the map.
Man:	Okay, I got it.
Woman:	Then put in the money.
Man:	Right, okay.
Woman:	After that, push the button for the ticket price.
Man:	Right, I see.
Woman:	Then take your ticket and change.

EXERCISE 3

Practice the conversation a few more times with your partner. Each time, use one of the the things below to ask for and give instructions.

Memo
- ALWAYS LOOK AT THE PERSON YOU ARE SPEAKING TO—DONT LOOK DOWN AT THE TEXT!
- YOU CAN ALSO ASK HOW TO USE OTHER THINGS.

VOCABULARY
- ATM
- copy machine
- fax machine

LISTENING TASK

EXERCISE 1

Listen to six conversations between a flight attendant and two passengers. Write the number of each conversation on the correct picture (1 through 6).

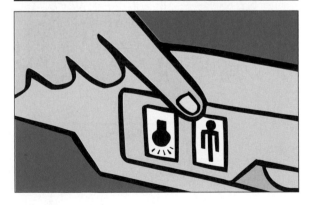

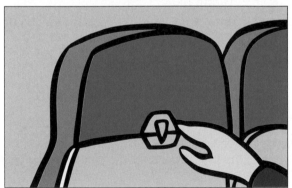

EXERCISE 2

Now listen to six *different* conversations between the two passengers, a husband and wife. On each of the pictures (1 through 6), write "**H**" if the husband is right, or "**W**" if the wife is right.

PAIR WORK

Do Exercise 1 with a partner, and Exercise 2 with everyone.

EXERCISE 1

The teacher will assign each pair of students a set of six pictures (set *A, B, C,* or *D*) from page 21 or 22.
Each pair should work together and write down instructions for their pictures—that is, how to use the machine.

A   *Copy machine*

VOCABULARY
• lid / cover	• select
• face down	• push / press
• glass	• start button

B   *Photo booth*

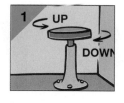

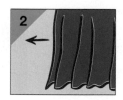

VOCABULARY
• adjust	• photo size
• curtain	• insert / put in
• select	• tray

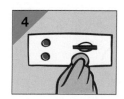

PAIR WORK

Do Exercise 2 with everyone.

EXERCISE 2

For each of the *other* three sets of pictures, walk around the classroom and find someone to give you the instructions, and write them below the pictures.

Example:

Student A: *Excuse me. Could you tell me how to use the photo booth?*

Student B: *Sure. First, you adjust the seat. Then you . . .*

Memo
• TALK TO ONE PERSON AT A TIME IN EXERCISE 2.
• LOOK AT THE PERSON WHEN YOU GIVE INSTRUCTIONS—DONT READ FROM THE PAGE.

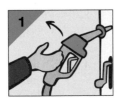

....
....
....

....
....
....

C   *Gasoline pump*

VOCABULARY
- nozzle
- insert / put in
- gas pump
- gas tank
- lever
- replace

D   *Coin laundry machine*

VOCABULARY
- laundry
- compartment
- pour
- select / set
- detergent
- insert / put in

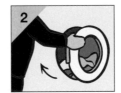

....
....

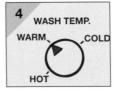
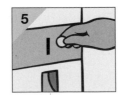

....
....
....

GROUP WORK *Do each exercise with a new group.*

EXERCISE 1

In groups of three, take turns doing the actions in the box.
Then think up six more actions and add them to the list.

ACTIONS		
crawl	pinch	squeeze
cry	point at	throw
frown at	pound on	tickle
grab	pull	turn around
hug	punch	wave to
jump	push	wink at
kick	scratch	....
kneel	scream at	....
laugh at	shake	....
lean on	skip	....
open	slap	....
pick up	smile at	

EXERCISE 2

Form *new* groups of three, and write a *silent movie scene*
for two people (*Student A* and *Student B*) who will each
act out six or more actions during the scene.
(Use actions in the box above or make up your own.)

Example:

Student A: *Point at the window and push Student B.*
Student B: *Go to the window and wink at Student A.*
Student A: *Go and stand behind Student B, turn around,
and cry.*

EXERCISE 3

Again, form new groups of three. Take turns being the
director of the movie scene that you wrote in *Exercise 2*,
giving instructions to the two *actors/actresses* (*Student A*
and *Student B*).

Example:

Director: *Carla, point at the window and push Michael.*
Carla: *[Points at the window and pushes Michael.]*
Director: *Good. Now, Michael, go to the window and
wink at Carla.*
Michael: *[Goes to the window and winks at Carla.]*
Director: *Okay. Carla, go and stand behind Michael,
turn around, and cry.*

5 SAY THAT AGAIN

WARM-UP EXERCISES   *Do Exercise 1 alone and Exercise 2 with a partner.*

EXERCISE 1

Below are four different conversations, and each conversation has four sentences (boxes 1 through 4).
Match the sentences on the left and right to make each conversation (*1, 2, 3,* and *4*).

Student A

Box 1

1 **How do you set the time on this?**

2 **Do you know when Flight 97 arrives?**

3 **Could you hold the elevator for me?**

4 **Your watch? What does it look like?**

Student B

Box 2

☐ **It's black, and it has four little buttons.**

☐ **Sure, I'd be glad to, Mrs. Olsen.**

☐ **Yes, it lands at 10:45, in ten minutes.**

1 **First, hold in this button on the side.**

Box 3

☐ **Would you mind pushing 6 for me?**

1 **Okay, the hour is blinking. Now what?**

☐ **Does it have numbers on the face?**

☐ **Could you tell me the gate number?**

Box 4

☐ **Yes, but just 12, 3, 6 and 9.**

☐ **Not at all—there you are.**

☐ **Yes, go to number 15.**

1 **Then push this button to change it.**

EXERCISE 2

Student A:

Choose *any* sentence in box 1 to begin—*1, 2, 3* or *4*—
and say the first sentence to *Student B.*
Then listen to *Student B* and say the next sentence.

Student B:

Listen to *Student A's* sentence and say the next
sentence to *Student A.*

Memo

• FOLD THE PAGE
AND LOOK ONLY
AT YOUR SIDE IN
EXERCISE 2.

LISTENING TASK

EXERCISE 1

Listen to the conversations (1 through 5) and write the number of each conversation on the correct picture.

EXERCISE 2

Listen again and write the *key words* next to each picture.

Memo

• KEY WORDS ARE IMPORTANT WORDS, OR WORDS THAT TELL YOU WHICH PICTURE TO CHOOSE.

PAIR WORK

Student A:

Choose any twelve objects in the office above.
  • Write the numbers 1 through 12 on the objects.
  • Then describe each object to *Student B,* and tell *Student B* how to use it.

Answer questions about each object until *Student B* guesses correctly what it is.

Student B:

Student A will describe twelve objects in the office, one at a time, and tell you how to use each one. Ask questions and guess what each object is.

Memo
  • STUDENT A: DON'T SAY WHAT EACH OBJECT IS, OR WHAT IT IS USED FOR.
  • DO THIS EXERCISE AGAIN—TAKE TURNS AS STUDENT A AND STUDENT B.

GROUP WORK   *Do Exercise 1 alone and Exercise 2 with everyone.*

EXERCISE 1

Circle any four of the things below: [**O**] *these are things you don't have and **want to borrow**.*
Make an "X" on four other things: [**X**] *these are things you have, but **cannot lend** to anyone.*
Leave four of the things unmarked: *these are things you have and **can lend**.*

EXERCISE 2

Walk around the classroom and try to borrow the four things you circled above [**O**].
  • Refuse to lend the things you marked with an "X," and *give a reason* for refusing.
  • Lend each unmarked thing to the first person who asks you. (You can only lend each thing <u>one</u> time.)

Examples:

Student A: *Do you think you could lend me your tennis racket?*
Student B: *I'm sorry, but my sister is using it.*

Student A: *Could you possibly lend me your bicycle this afternoon?*
Student C: *Sure, no problem.*

> **Memo**
> • TRY TO BORROW
> THINGS FROM FOUR
> <u>DIFFERENT</u> PEOPLE.
> • DO NOT LOOK
> AT ANYONE'S THINGS–
> JUST ASK AND ANSWER.

LANGUAGE GAME

Play this game with two to four "players" and one "caller".

Player

CALLER: LOOK AT PAGE 80

Take turns choosing two numbers (1 through 24) from the grid below.
Each number is a question or an answer. The caller will read each sentence that you choose.
Choose one number, listen to the caller read the sentence, and then choose another number.
Try to match a question with the answer.

Do not write any notes—*just listen!*

1	2	3	4	5	6
7	8	9	10	11	12
13	14	15	16	17	18
19	20	21	22	23	24

Continue until all the questions and answers have been matched.
The player with the most matches is the *winner!*

Memo

• CHECK (√) THE NUMBERS THAT <u>YOU</u> MATCH.
• CROSS OFF (X) THE NUMBERS THAT <u>ANOTHER PLAYER</u> MATCHES.
• LOOK AT THIS PAGE ONLY!

UNIT 5

WARM-UP EXERCISES

EXERCISE 1

Write a question in the empty speech balloon.

?

I'm sorry, but I have to use it.

EXERCISE 2

Practice the following conversation with a partner. (Take turns as *Alice* and *Mary*.)

Alice:	Hi, Mary. Nice day, isn't it?
Mary:	Yes, it is, Alice.
Alice:	Listen, Mary, can I borrow some sugar?
Mary:	Of course. Come on in.
Alice:	Could I also borrow your large mixing bowl?
Mary:	Well, sure, go ahead.
Alice:	And I wonder if I could use your oven?
Mary:	My oven? Sorry, I'm afraid I have to use it today.

EXERCISE 3

Practice the conversation a few more times with your partner.
Each time, talk about three of the items below. (Use your real name.)

VOCABULARY
- hammer
- ladder
- laptop
- pen
- textbook
- TV
- videocamera
- videotape
- pickup truck

LISTENING TASK

EXERCISE 1

Listen to the conversations (1 through 10) and write the number of each conversation on the correct picture.

EXERCISE 2

Listen to each conversation again. For each one (1 through 10), make a check (√) in the box for *Permission given* or *Permission refused*.

	Permission:		Reply:
	given	refused	
1.	☐	☐	....
2.	☐	☐	....
3.	☐	☐	....
4.	☐	☐	....
5.	☐	☐	....
6.	☐	☐	....
7.	☐	☐	....
8.	☐	☐	....
9.	☐	☐	....
10.	☐	☐	....

EXERCISE 3

Listen to each conversation once more. Make a note of the *reply* in each one (1 through 10).

Memo

• IN EXERCISE 3, YOU CAN WRITE A SHORT SENTENCE OR JUST A FEW WORDS.

PAIR WORK

Example:

Student A: *Is it okay if I wear your new sweater on a date?*

Student B: *Sure, go ahead.*

EXERCISE 1

You are a college student. *Student B* is your roommate. Ask *Student B* if you can:

• wear *Student B's* new sweater on a date.

• watch a movie on TV tonight.

• use *Student B's* computer to do some homework.

• have a small party next Saturday night.

• use *Student B's* camera this weekend.

• invite a few friends over to play cards.

• borrow *Student B's* car Friday night.

• take *Student B's* CD player to the beach.

Check (√):
*Permission
given refused*

EXERCISE 2

You are *Student B's* boss.
Student B is an office worker.
Look at the information in the box.
Answer *Student B's* requests.
(You can give or refuse permission.)

Student B is a very good worker. You usually say "Yes" to *Student B's* requests, but remember these things:
• The company car can only be used for business.
• There's an important company meeting early Monday morning.
• This summer you want all the workers to take short vacations.

EXERCISE 3

You are a student. *Student B* is your teacher.
Ask *Student B* for permission to:

• borrow *Student B's* dictionary.

• leave class early today.

• hand in the book report one day late.

• come to class late tomorrow.

• change the subject of your history report.

• go to the rest room.

• take a make-up test for the exam you missed.

• miss class on Monday.

Check (√):
*Permission
given refused*

EXERCISE 4

You are *Student B's* mother/father.
Student B is a teenager.
Look at the information in the box.
Answer *Student B's* requests.
(You can give or refuse permission.)

Student B is a good son/daughter. You usually say "Yes" to *Student B's* requests, but remember these things:
• *Student B* has to study more after school and in the evening.
• You hate motorcycles—they're too dangerous.
• *Student B* is too young to go on a trip overseas with friends.

GROUP WORK   *Do this exercise with everyone.*

The teacher will give you *one* of the boxes on page 32 or 33.
Walk around the classroom and ask for permission and give permission.
Write the name of the person who gives permission in each blank.

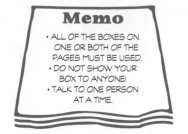

Memo
· ALL OF THE BOXES ON
ONE OR BOTH OF THE
PAGES MUST BE USED.
· DO NOT SHOW YOUR
BOX TO ANYONE!
· TALK TO ONE PERSON
AT A TIME.

Example:
Student A: *Would it be possible for me to borrow your car?*
Student B: *Sure.*

1

Ask for permission to:

• borrow your friend's car.

name

• open a window.

name

• turn down the radio.

name

- -

Give permission to:

• turn on the light.

• borrow your textbook.

• take your picture.

Refuse all other requests!

2

Ask for permission to:

• use your friend's computer.

name

• close the door.

name

• borrow your friend's textbook.

name

- -

Give permission to:

• turn down the radio.

• use your telephone.

• borrow your sweater.

Refuse all other requests!

3

Ask for permission to:

• take your friend's picture.

name

• borrow your friend's sweater.

name

• turn off the TV.

name

- -

Give permission to:

• use your computer.

• open a window.

• borrow your bicycle.

Refuse all other requests!

4

Ask for permission to:

• borrow your friend's bicycle.

name

• turn on the light.

name

• use your friend's telephone.

name

- -

Give permission to:

• borrow your car.

• close the door.

• turn off the TV.

Refuse all other requests!

Example:

Student B: *Okay if I close a window?*

Student C: *Well, I'd rather you didn't.*

5

Ask for permission to:

• use your friend's surfboard. ....
  name

• close a window. ....
  name

• turn on the TV. ....
  name

- -

Give permission to:

• play with your friend's dog.

• borrow your skis.

• watch a movie on TV.

Refuse all other requests!

6

Ask for permission to:

• turn up the heat. ....
  name

• read your friend's diary. ....
  name

• borrow your friend's skis. ....
  name

- -

Give permission to:

• turn on the TV.

• use your motorcycle.

• turn off the light.

Refuse all other requests!

7

Ask for permission to:

• watch a movie on TV. ....
  name

• turn off the light. ....
  name

• borrow your friend's boat. ....
  name

- -

Give permission to:

• turn up the heat.

• close a window.

• open the door.

Refuse all other requests!

8

Ask for permission to:

• open the door. ....
  name

• play with your friend's dog. ....
  name

• use your friend's motorcycle. ....
  name

- -

Give permission to:

• use your surfboard.

• read your diary.

• borrow your boat.

Refuse all other requests!

7 EXCUSES, EXCUSES

WARM-UP EXERCISES

EXERCISE 1

Write one or two sentences in the empty speech balloon.

EXERCISE 2

Practice the following conversation with a partner. (Take turns as *Ann* and *Lou*.)

Ann: Where were you? I waited for two hours last night!

Lou: I'm sorry, Ann, but I had to drive to the airport.

Ann: Why didn't you call me?

Lou: Oh, well, I couldn't find your office phone number.

Ann: Oh. So why didn't you call me at home later?

Lou: Well, I forgot.

Ann: Well, next time, don't forget!

Lou: I'm really sorry, Ann.

EXERCISE 3

Practice the conversation a few more times with your partner. Each time, use the excuses below (1 through 3).

1. had to go to the hospital

2. didn't have change for the telephone

3. fell asleep

1. had to go to a business meeting

2. didn't have time

3. got home too late

Memo

• ALWAYS LOOK AT THE PERSON YOU ARE SPEAKING TO—DON'T LOOK DOWN AT THE TEXT!

• YOU CAN ALSO MAKE UP YOUR OWN EXCUSES.

LISTENING TASK

EXERCISE 1

Listen to the conversation and circle Jonathan's excuses.

EXERCISE 2

Listen to the conversation again. Next to each of the excuses, make a "√" if Mrs. Fenway believes the excuse, or an "X" if she doesn't believe it.

EXERCISE 3

After you listen to the conversation once more, look at the pictures and make a note of each of Jonathan's excuses.

PAIR WORK

STUDENT B:
LOOK AT
PAGE 82

EXERCISE 1

You are a teacher. *Student B* is a student. Ask
Student B questions. Write down *Student B's* excuses.

Example:

Student A: *Why didn't you finish the test yesterday?*
Student B: *I couldn't remember the answers.*

Student B didn't...	*Student B's* excuse:
• finish the test yesterday.	
• come to class on Monday.	
• bring any books to class today.	
• come to class on time.	
• finish writing the book report.	
• do the homework.	

EXERCISE 2

You are a teenager. *Student B* is your mother/father.
Listen to each question and give *Student B* an excuse.
(Use *"I couldn't..."* or *"I had to..."* with the cues below.)

- ...find the vacuum cleaner.
- ...study for an English test.
- ...pick up the garbage can—it was too heavy!
- ...find the dog food.
- ...*(make up your own excuse)*
- ...*(make up your own excuse)*

EXERCISE 3

You did not do any of the six things below (1 through 6).
- Write down a reason for each thing you didn't do (1 through 6).
- Walk around the classroom and ask for and give reasons for each one (1 through 6).
  Write down the name of one person who has a *similar* reason next to each one.

You didn't...	Your reason:	
1. go bowling Friday night.		name
2. go swimming on Saturday.		name
3. go to the big party Saturday night.		name
4. play ball Sunday morning.		name
5. go shopping on Sunday.		name
6. go to the movies Sunday night.		name

UNIT 7

GROUP WORK *Do Exercise 1 alone and Exercise 2 with your group.*

EXERCISE 1

Write the numbers of all the activities (1 through 16) in any order on your grid below.

1
2
3
4
5
6
7
8

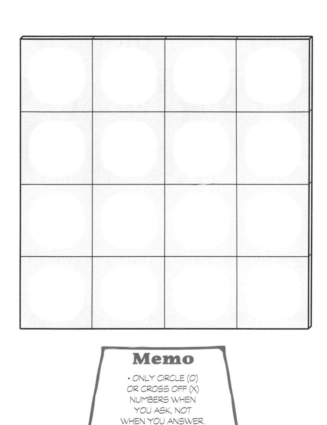

Memo
• ONLY CIRCLE (O) OR CROSS OFF (X) NUMBERS WHEN YOU ASK, NOT WHEN YOU ANSWER.
• KEEP TRACK OF YOUR ANSWERS (YES OR NO).

9
10
11
12
13
14
15
16

EXERCISE 2

Take turns asking each other about the activities. When it's your turn, you can ask *any* student in your group.
- **Ask,** and circle (**O**) any activity on your grid that the student did, and cross off (**X**) any activity that the student did not do.
- When you **answer,** you can say "yes" or "no" to any question, but <u>you must give a reason if you say "no."</u>

Continue until all your numbers are marked. Each time you get four **O**'s or four **X**'s in a line, shout *"Bingo!"* The student with the most "bingos" is the winner!

Examples:

Student A: *John, did you go to school last Friday?*
Student B: *Yes, I did.*

Student B: *Mary, did you fix your bicycle yesterday?*
Student C: *No, I didn't. I couldn't find the tools.*

UNIT 7

37

8 COULDN'T AGREE MORE

GIVING OPINIONS

WARM-UP EXERCISES

EXERCISE 1

Write one or two sentences in each empty speech balloon.

EXERCISE 2

Practice the following conversation with *two* other students. (Take turns as *Tim, Eri,* and *Jay.*)

Tim: **I don't think surprise quizzes are fair.**
Eri: **I agree with you, Tim.**
Jay: **Actually, I think they're okay, if you study every day.**

Tim: **In my opinion, all tests are useless.**
Eri: **I think so, too.**
Jay: **I don't think so. Tests make us work hard and learn.**

EXERCISE 3

Practice the conversation a few more times in groups of three.
Student A: give an opinion (below).
Student B: agree.
Student C: disagree and give a reason (below).

Memo

- ALWAYS LOOK AT THE PERSON YOU ARE SPEAKING TO–DONT LOOK DOWN AT THE TEXT!
- YOU CAN ALSO GIVE YOUR OWN OPINION IN THE CONVERSATION.

Student A - *Opinion*	***Student B*** - *Agree*	***Student C*** - *Disagree/reason*
...watching television is a waste of time	...	*...there are some good things on TV.*
...teachers give too much homework.	...	*...homework helps students to learn.*
...females are better at learning a foreign language.	...	*...males in this class are as good as the females.*

LISTENING TASK 🎧

EXERCISE 1

Each picture shows an opinion.
Listen to the conversation and write
a number on each to show the order
that the opinions are given (1 through 3).

EXERCISE 2

Listen to the conversation again and
for each picture, circle (**O**) the name of
the person who gives the opinion.

EXERCISE 3

Listen again and check (√) the names
of the people who agree or disagree
with each opinion.

Opinion:	Bob	John	Sue	Mary
Agree:				
Disagree:				

Opinion:	Bob	John	Sue	Mary
Agree:				
Disagree:				

Opinion:	Bob	John	Sue	Mary
Agree:				
Disagree:				

PAIR WORK

Do Exercises 1 and 3 alone, and Exercises 2 and 4 with a partner.

UNIT 8

EXERCISE 1

Match each opinion
on page 40
with a reason to
agree below.

Memo
• IN EXERCISE 2,
GIVE OPINIONS
AND AGREE
IN DIFFERENT WAYS.
(LOOK ONLY AT
PAGE 40 OR PAGE 41.)

EXERCISE 2

With a partner, take turns giving opinions and agreeing.
One student give an opinion from page 40, and the
other student agree and give a reason from below.

Examples:

Student A: *I think zoos are cruel places.*
Student B: *That's true. I believe that animals shouldn't be
kept in cages.*

Student B: *In my opinion, there's too much violence on TV.*
Student A: *I agree with you. I think it has a bad effect
on young people.*

The air is dirty and there's too much noise.

There's nothing to do,
and there's no privacy.

It helps you to see
your own country and
culture more clearly.

Animals shouldn't be kept in cages.

It's wrong to
ignore them.

The government should provide
free education for everyone.

They are bad for the country's health.

It would help to improve
international relations.

It has a bad effect
on young people.

You can buy things
anytime, anywhere.

EXERCISE 3

Match each opinion
on page 40
with a reason to
disagree below.

Memo
• IN EXERCISE 4,
GIVE OPINIONS
AND DISAGREE
IN DIFFERENT WAYS.
(LOOK ONLY AT
PAGE 40 OR PAGE 41.)

EXERCISE 4

With a partner, take turns giving opinions and disagreeing.
One student give an opinion from page 40, and the other
student disagree and give a reason from below.

Examples:

Student A: *I think zoos are cruel places.*
Student B: *Actually, I think the animals
are usually treated very well.*

Student B: *In my opinion, there's too much violence on TV.*
Student A: *I don't think so. I believe they only put on what
people want to watch.*

There's so much to do — such as going
to plays and the opera, and visiting
museums and art galleries.

You can learn just as
much traveling around
your *own* country.

Helping them find jobs
and their own places to live
is more important.

It's so difficult—I think learning *one* is enough.

It's too easy to spend
more than you have.

People are friendly
and there's less crime.

They only put on
what people want
to watch.

They are not *all* terrible—
some serve good food.

It gives parents and students more choice.

The animals are
usually treated very well.

GROUP WORK   *Do this exercise in groups of three.*

EXERCISE 1

Write the five topics (from your box on the right) in boxes 1 through 5 on page 43, and make up a topic for box 6.

Then take turns interviewing each other about the topics. Make notes of your partners' answers in each box.

Example:

Student A: *Keiko, what do you think about watching sports on TV?*
Student B: *I think it's a waste of time.*
Student A: *Do you agree, Juan?*
Student C: *No, I think it's a great way to relax.*

Memo
• STUDENTS WHO ARE ANSWERING QUESTIONS SHOULD CLOSE THE BOOK.
• DON'T JUST SAY YOU LIKE OR DISLIKE SOMETHING —GIVE AN OPINION.

EXERCISE 2   (OPTIONAL)

The teacher may call on you to tell the class about your partners' opinions on one of your topics. Look at your notes and tell the class what your partners said.

Example:

Teacher: *Ivan, what do your partners think about watching sports on TV?*
Ivan: *Keiko thinks watching sports on TV is a waste of time, but Juan disagrees. He thinks it's a great way to relax.*

Student A: Interview *Student B* and *Student C* about the topics in this box:

1. Watching sports on TV
2. Foreign movies
3. Loud parties
4. Traveling by bus
5. Learning to speak English
6. (Make up a topic)

Student B: Interview *Student A* and *Student C* about the topics in this box:

1. TV game shows
2. The Internet
3. Surprise parties
4. Traveling by train
5. Doing English homework
6. (Make up a topic)

Student C: Interview *Student A* and *Student B* about the topics in this box:

1. TV talk shows
2. Video games
3. Karaoke parties
4. Traveling by plane
5. This group work exercise
6. (Make up a topic)

Write each topic (1 through 6) in a box below.
Make notes of your partners answers below each topic.

Memo
• YOU CAN AGREE OR DISAGREE WITH YOUR PARTNER, BUT GIVE A REASON.

1.

2.

3.

4.

5.

6.

9 BIGGER AND BETTER

WARM-UP EXERCISES

EXERCISE 1

Write one or two sentences in the second speech balloon.

My dog is cuter than your dog.

Oh yeah?

EXERCISE 2

Practice the following conversation with a partner. (Take turns as *Fran* and *Larry*.)

Fran:	**You like motorcycles more than cars?**
Larry:	**Sure, why not?**
Fran:	**Well, a motorcycle is more dangerous than a car.**
Larry:	**True, but a car isn't as enjoyable as a motorcycle.**
Fran:	**Maybe, but is a motorcycle as comfortable as a car?**
Larry:	**No, it's not—but it's cheaper and easier to park.**
Fran:	**Okay, but which is better in bad weather?**
Larry:	**That's a good point.**

EXERCISE 3

Practice the conversation a few more times with your partner. Each time, compare two things below.

VOCABULARY
- *city*
- *country*
- *desktop computer*
- *laptop*
- *TV*
- *movie theater*

Memo
- ALWAYS LOOK AT THE PERSON YOU ARE SPEAKING TO— DONT LOOK DOWN AT THE TEXT!
- YOU CAN ALSO MAKE COMPARISONS ABOUT OTHER THINGS.

LISTENING TASK 🎧

EXERCISE 1

Listen to the conversations (1 through 5) and check (√) the correct picture for each one.

1 ☐ ☐

2 ☐ ☐

3 ☐ ☐

4 ☐ ☐

5 ☐ ☐

EXERCISE 2

Listen again and write the number of each conversation (1 through 5) on any of the words that are used in comparisons.

☐ long	☐ delicious	☐ nice	☐ big
☐ comfortable	☐ handsome	☐ cheap	☐ roomy
☐ sporty	☐ good	☐ mature	☐ expensive

EXERCISE 3

Listen once more and complete each of the following sentences using one of the words from *Exercise 2*. Then compare sentences with a partner.

1. The white ones are ....

2. The red one is ....

3. The one on the right is ....

4. The Phuket tour is ....

5. The woman thinks hers is ....

PAIR WORK

Student A:

Choose one of the groups of pictures below (on page 46 or 47), but don't tell *Student B* which one.

Student B will ask you questions about comparisons with the items at the top to find out which group you picked.

Example:

Student B: *Is your car as expensive as a BMW?*

Student A: *No, it's not.*

car

movie

restaurant

BMW

Group A
Picasso
Ford

Group B
Ferrari
LUIGI'S
Leonardo

Group E
Ferrari
LUIGI'S
Picasso

Group F
Ford
ALIEN
LUIGI'S
Leonardo

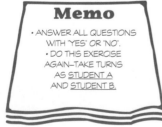
Memo

• ANSWER ALL QUESTIONS WITH 'YES' OR 'NO'.
• DO THIS EXERCISE AGAIN—TAKE TURNS AS <u>STUDENT A</u> AND <u>STUDENT B</u>.

chair  instrument  painting

van Gogh

Student B:

Find out which group of pictures *Student A* has chosen by asking "yes/no" questions, comparing the items in groups below with the ones at the top (on pages 46 and 47).

Example:

Student B: Is your movie more romantic than Star Wars?

Student A: Yes, it is.

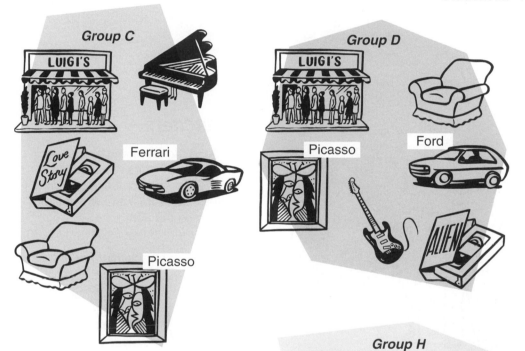

Group C

LUIGI'S

Ferrari

Picasso

Group D

LUIGI'S

Picasso

Ford

Group G

Ford

Leonardo

Group H

JIMMY'S HAMBURGERS

Leonardo

Ferrari

VOCABULARY

- big
- busy
- cheap
- comfortable
- crowded
- economical
- exciting
- expensive
- fast
- loud
- modern
- nice
- old
- popular
- romantic
- scary
- slow
- small
- soft
- valuable

Memo

• BEGIN ALL YOUR QUESTIONS: "IS YOUR (CAR)...?" DON'T ASK: "IS IT (A FORD?)"

GROUP WORK Do Exercise 1 alone and Exercise 2 with everyone.

EXERCISE 1

Look at the differences between the two pictures. Choose six differences and write a comparison for each on the lines below.

Example:
The yard was dirtier ten years ago.

Memo
• IN YOUR SENTENCES USE "MORE/~ER TEN YEARS AGO" OR "MORE/~ER TODAY."

Ten years ago

Today

EXERCISE 2

Go around the class and exchange comparisons. For each one of your comparisons, find someone who made a *similar* comparison and write his or her name on the right.

Example:

Joe: The yard was dirtier ten years ago.

May: Right, the yard is cleaner today.

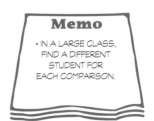

Memo
• IN A LARGE CLASS, FIND A DIFFERENT STUDENT FOR EACH COMPARISON.

Comparison	Student's name

10 SAY THAT AGAIN

WARM-UP EXERCISES

Do Exercise 1 alone and Exercise 2 with a partner.

EXERCISE 1

Below are four different conversations, and each conversation has four sentences (boxes 1 through 4).
Match the sentences on the left and right to make each conversation (*1, 2, 3,* and *4*).

Student A

Box 1

1. **I wonder if I could borrow your car?**
2. **I think the air in this city is too dirty.**
3. **Why didn't you pick up Jill from work?**
4. **Jogging is healthier than cycling.**

Student B

Box 2

- [ ] **I agree. There are too many cars.**
- [ ] **Yeah, but riding a bicycle is more fun.**
- [ ] **I'm sorry, but I have to use it today.**
- [ ] **I had to fix the car.**

Box 3

- [ ] **Did you tell her to take the bus home?**
- [ ] **Well, do you mind if I use it tomorrow?**
- [ ] **Which is more popular for exercise?**
- [ ] **I believe we all should use the subway.**

Box 4

- [ ] **I think more people go jogging.**
- [ ] **Oh, no! I forgot!**
- [ ] **Actually, I think that buses are better.**
- [ ] **Not at all.**

EXERCISE 2

Student A:

Choose *any* sentence in box 1 to begin—*1, 2, 3* or *4*—
and say the first sentence to *Student B*.
Then listen to *Student B* and say the next sentence.

Student B:

Listen to *Student A's* sentence and say the next
sentence to *Student A*.

Memo

• FOLD THE PAGE
AND LOOK ONLY AT
YOUR SIDE
IN EXERCISE 2.

LISTENING TASK 🎧

EXERCISE 1

Listen to the conversations (1 through 5) and write the number
of each conversation on the correct picture.

EXERCISE 2

Listen again and write the *key words* next to each picture.

Memo
• KEY WORDS ARE
IMPORTANT WORDS,
OR WORDS THAT TELL
YOU WHICH PICTURE
TO CHOOSE.

PAIR WORK

EXERCISE 1

Write a comparison for each picture (1 through 4):   Write a request for permission for each picture (5 through 8):

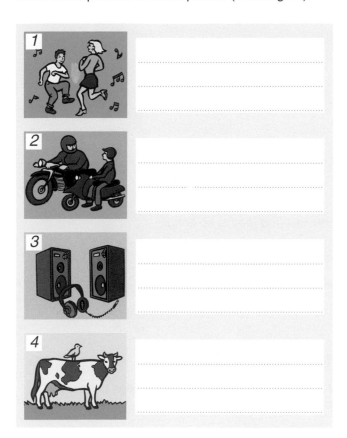

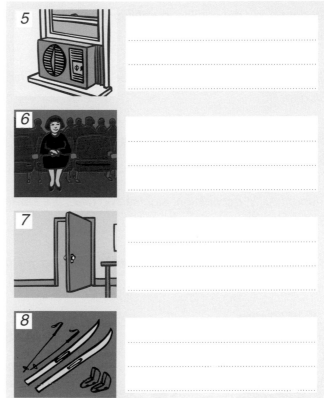

EXERCISE 2

Take turns with *Student B* guessing what each other wrote for each picture in *Exercise 1*.
These are *Student B's* pictures from *Exercise 1*:

Comparisons   *Requests for permission*

Memo
• EACH STUDENT
CAN MAKE ONLY
ONE GUESS PER TURN.
• THE WORDING DOES
NOT HAVE TO BE
EXACTLY THE SAME.

*The first one to guess
all eight correctly
is the winner!*

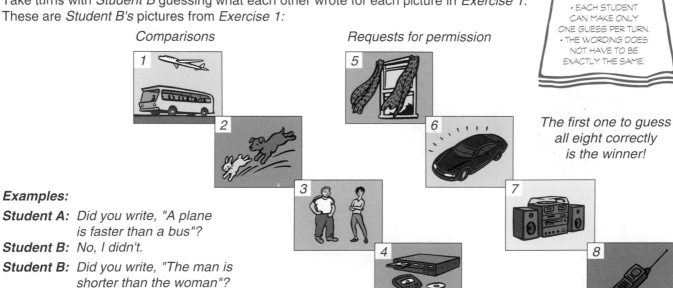

Examples:

Student A: *Did you write, "A plane
is faster than a bus"?*

Student B: *No, I didn't.*

Student B: *Did you write, "The man is
shorter than the woman"?*

Student A: *Yes, I did.*

PAIR WORK

EXERCISE 3

Tell *Student B* your opinions (1 through 5) and write down *Student B's* reply to each one.

1   Student A: *In my opinion, gambling should be illegal.*
     Student B: ....

2   Student A: *I think English is harder to learn than Chinese.*
     Student B: ....

3   Student A: *I believe there's too much violence on TV.*
     Student B: ....

4   Student A: *In my opinion, sightseeing tours are a waste of time—and they're so tiring!*
     Student B: ....

5   Student A: *I don't think people should spend so much money on weddings.*
     Student B: ....

EXERCISE 4

Listen to *Student B's* opinions. Use one of the replies below to agree or disagree with *Student B*.

    (DISAGREE) + "I think it's boring."

    (AGREE) + "I couldn't do anything without mine!"

    (DISAGREE) + "Many of them have very short careers."

    (AGREE) + "They get old and can have mechanical problems."

Memo

• USE DIFFERENT
EXPRESSIONS
TO AGREE
OR DISAGREE.

    (AGREE) + "I like to see my teacher face to face."

EXERCISE 5

Discuss all the topics with your partner, giving your <u>own</u> opinions.

GROUP WORK *Do this exercise in a group of four or more students.*

The first student must choose a picture and say *why* he didn't do it.
The next student must repeat the statement and then choose a different picture and make one more statement.
Each student must repeat *every* previous statement and make one more statement using a new picture.

Continue around the circle and use as many pictures as possible, repeating *all* the statements—with names—for about fifteen minutes (until your teacher says "stop").

Examples:

Memo
• DO NOT WRITE ANYTHING ON THE PICTURES.
• HELP EACH OTHER REPEAT THE STATEMENTS.

James: I didn't exercise because I got up late.
(Student A)

Yuko: James didn't exercise because he got up late.
(Student B) I didn't do laundry because I had to study.

Vera: James didn't exercise because he got up late. Yuko didn't do laundry
(Student C) because she had to study. I didn't call because I forgot.

James: I didn't exercise because I got up late. Yuko didn't do laundry
(Student A) because she had to study. Vera didn't call because she forgot.
I didn't get a haircut because. . .

(continue)

The group of students who use the most pictures—and correctly repeat the most statements—are the winners!

LANGUAGE GAME

Play this game with two to four "players" and one "caller".

Player

CALLER: LOOK AT PAGE 85

Take turns choosing two numbers (1 through 24) from the grid below.
Each number is a question or an answer. The caller will read each sentence that you choose.
Choose one number, listen to the caller read the sentence, and then choose another number.
Try to match a question with the answer.

Do not write any notes—*just listen!*

(1)	(2)	(3)	(4)	(5)	(6)
(7)	(8)	(9)	(10)	(11)	(12)
(13)	(14)	(15)	(16)	(17)	(18)
(19)	(20)	(21)	(22)	(23)	(24)

Continue until all the questions and answers have been matched.
The player with the most matches is the *winner!*

Memo
• CHECK (√) THE NUMBERS THAT YOU MATCH.
• CROSS OFF (X) THE NUMBERS THAT ANOTHER PLAYER MATCHES.
• LOOK AT THIS PAGE ONLY!

11 IF I WERE YOU

WARM-UP EXERCISES

EXERCISE 1

Write one or two sentences in the empty speech balloon.

EXERCISE 2

Practice the following conversation with a partner. (Take turns as *Rick* and *Greg*.)

Rick: What's the matter, Greg?

Greg: I want to go fishing with friends on Sunday, but I have to work.

Rick: Did you tell your boss that?

Greg: No. He just asked everyone to work.

Rick: Why don't you tell him you have an upset stomach on Sunday?

Greg: No, I couldn't do that.

Rick: Then you should just tell him you made plans.

Greg: Right, maybe I will.

EXERCISE 3

Practice the conversation a few more times with your partner. Each time, use a different plan and different advice below.

Memo

• ALWAYS LOOK AT THE PERSON YOU ARE SPEAKING TO—DONT LOOK DOWN AT THE TEXT!
• YOU CAN ALSO MAKE UP YOUR OWN PLANS AND ADVICE.

LISTENING TASK 🎧

EXERCISE 1

Listen to the conversation and circle the
things that are suggested to Elizabeth.

EXERCISE 2

Listen to the conversation again.
Next to each of the suggestions, write
a "√ " if Elizabeth accepts the idea,
a "?" if she *may* accept the idea, or
an "X" if she rejects the idea.

PAIR WORK

EXERCISE 1

Student B has a problem.
- Listen and ask *Student B*: "What's wrong?" or "What's the matter?"
- Listen to *Student B's* problems and give *Student B* advice.

Choose advice to give *Student B* from the pictures below.

Memo
- GIVE ADVICE IN DIFFERENT WAYS.
- MAKE UP YOUR OWN ADVICE FOR ONE PROBLEM.

Example:

Student B: *Oh, no!*
Student A: *What's the matter?*
Student B: *I lost my ATM card!*
Student A: *You'd better call the bank.*

(Make up your own advice)

EXERCISE 2

You have a problem.
- Tell *Student B* your problems (1 through 7).
  (Begin by saying something like "Oh no!" or "Ohhh....")
- Write down *Student B's* advice below each problem.

Memo
- MAKE UP ONE PROBLEM (#7).
- THE TEACHER MAY GIVE YOU DIFFERENT EXPRESSIONS TO BEGIN YOUR CONVERSATION.

1. You left your camera on the train.

2. You only slept two hours last night.

3. You lost your passport.

4. You have a cold and a sore throat.

5. You locked your keys in your car.

6. You have a toothache.

7. *(make up a problem)*

PAIR WORK

EXERCISE 3

Student B is taking a trip to Hong Kong.
Listen to the plans and give *Student B* advice.
Choose advice from the pictures below,
or make up your own advice.

Example:

Student B: *I'm going to stay at the Excelsior Hotel.*
Do you think that's a good idea?
Student A: *Why don't you stay at the YMCA?*
It's much cheaper.

the YMCA

a sightseeing tour

traveler's checks

the ferry and subway

Make up your own advice

Memo
• DO EXERCISE 4
TWICE—TAKE TURNS
AS <u>STUDENT A</u> AND
<u>STUDENT B</u>.

EXERCISE 4

Student B will tell you the name of a place that *Student B* knows well.
• Tell *Student B* that you are going to take a trip to this place on vacation next summer.
• Ask for *Student B's* advice about a good place to stay, places to go sightseeing, etc.,
and make notes on the memo pad.

Example:

Student B: *I grew up in Singapore.*
Student A: *Oh, really? I'm going there on*
vacation next summer! Listen,
could you tell me...

memo

POSSIBLE THINGS TO ASK ABOUT
• A good place to stay   • Good places to eat
• Places to go sightseeing   • Things to do
• How to get around   • Things to buy

GROUP WORK *Do Exercise 1 alone and Exercise 2 with everyone.*

EXERCISE 1

Read what each person says (1 through 5) and write down some advice below each picture.

EXERCISE 2

Walk around the classroom and talk about each problem (1 through 5), and your advice for each one. Above each problem, write the name of someone with advice *similar* to yours.

Example:
Student A: *John bought a used car last week and now it won't start.*
Student B: *He ought to bring it to a repair shop.*
Student A: *If I were him, I'd . . .*

> **Memo**
> • KEEP CHANGING PARTNERS.

3
> I have to study for a big test on Monday, but I've been invited to a birthday party on Saturday and a beach party on Sunday.

Sharon

....

....

1
> Last night I saw my girlfriend at the movies on a date with my best friend.

Pete

....

....

....

4
> I have the lead in the school play tomorrow but I have a bad cold.

Martin

....

....

....

2
> I bought a used car last week and now it won't start.

John

....

....

....

5
> On the train this morning I found a paper bag with $500 in it!

Angela

....

....

....

12 HAVE YOU EVER?

WARM-UP EXERCISES

EXERCISE 1

Write one or two sentences in the empty speech balloon.

Have you ever had a car accident?

EXERCISE 2

Practice the following conversation with a partner. (Take turns as *Tama* and *Hiro*.)

Tama: Have you ever been bungy-jumping?

Hiro: No, I haven't. Have you?

Tama: Yeah, I went with my boyfriend last year.

Hiro: Really? What was it like?

Tama: It was fantastic—I loved it!

Hiro: Where did you do it?

Tama: In Canada. Have you ever been there?

Hiro: Yes, I went to Quebec five years ago, on vacation.

Memo

• ALWAYS LOOK AT THE PERSON YOU ARE SPEAKING TO—DON'T LOOK DOWN AT THE TEXT!
• YOU CAN ALSO USE OTHER SPORTS/PLACES IN THE CONVERSATION.

EXERCISE 3

Practice the conversation a few more times with your partner. Each time, use an activity and place below when you ask or answer questions.

Switzerland

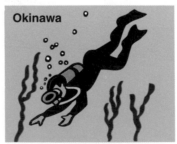

Okinawa

Colorado

LISTENING TASK

EXERCISE 1

Memo
• YOU CAN TAKE NOTES WHILE YOU LISTEN TO THE STORY.

• Look at the pictures, and then listen to the conversation with your book closed.
• Open you book and number the pictures in the correct order, according to Linda's story.

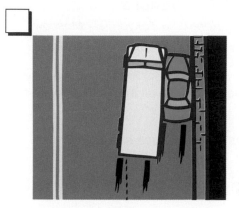

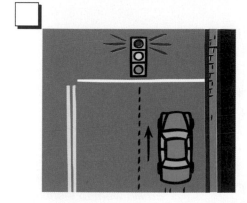

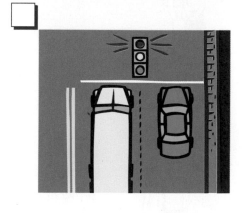

EXERCISE 2

Listen again and write the *key words* next to each picture.

PAIR WORK

Take turns with *Student B* asking and answering questions about the people below. For the empty boxes, find out:
- *where* they have been (ask about places in the box below)
- *when* they went there
- *why* they went

Memo
- DO NOT READ THE SENTENCES TO STUDENT B– JUST ANSWER THE QUESTIONS!

PLACES		
• Hong Kong	• Tokyo	• Moscow
• Senegal	• Nepal	• Cairo

First write *notes* of the answers next to each empty box, and later write one sentence with all the information *in* each box.

Example:

Student A: *Has Kurt ever been to Hong Kong?*
Student B: *No, he hasn't.*

(Afterwards compare sentences with your partner.)

Katrina

Kurt

Last year Jim flew to Australia with some friends to take part in a surfing competition.
Jim

Emilio went to Vienna, Austria three years ago to study music in a famous music school.
Emilio

Jack & Eri

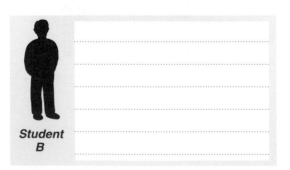
Student B

Debbie and Tom drove from New York City to Aspen, Colorado to go skiing in January.
Debbie & Tom

GROUP WORK *Do Exercise 1 alone and Exercise 2 with everyone.*

EXERCISE 1

Choose three of the topics below and make up a
"Have you ever ~ ?" question for each one.
Write a *specific* question on a pad on the right.

Example:

• *(a movie) Have you ever seen "E.T."?*

EXERCISE 2

Ask around the class and—for each question—
find someone who answers "Yes" and write down
his or her name. Then ask a few more question
about the experience and write down the details
(when, where, why, etc.).

TOPICS
• a movie
• a strange experience
• music
• a job
• language learning
• losing something
• foreign travel
• *(your own topic)*

Memo
• TALK TO THREE
DIFFERENT PEOPLE.
• TAKE TURNS ASKING
AND ANSWERING
QUESTIONS.

Topic: _____
Question: _____

Name: _____
Details: _____
_____
_____
_____
_____
_____

Topic: _____
Question: _____

Name: _____
Details: _____
_____
_____
_____
_____

Topic: _____
Question: _____

Name: _____
Details: _____
_____
_____
_____
_____
_____

EXERCISE 3   (OPTIONAL)

The teacher may call on you to tell the class about
one of the experiences you've asked about.
Look at your notes on the details of the experience
and tell the class the story.

13 HOW ABOUT DINNER?

WARM-UP EXERCISES

EXERCISE 1

Write one or two sentences in the empty speech balloon.

EXERCISE 2

Practice the following conversation with a partner. (Take turns as *Jade* and *Lena*.)

Jade:	Hi, Lena. Sit over here.
Lena:	Hi, Jade. Listen, would you like to see a movie tonight?
Jade:	I'm sorry, but I have to baby-sit.
Lena:	Oh. Then how about tomorrow night?
Jade:	Yeah, that sounds great—let's go tomorrow!
Lena:	Great! Let's meet at the bus stop after school.
Jade:	Sure, okay.
Lena:	So, what movie do you want to see?

Memo

• ALWAYS LOOK AT THE PERSON YOU ARE SPEAKING TO—DON'T LOOK DOWN AT THE TEXT!
• YOU CAN ALSO USE OTHER ACTIVITIES IN THE CONVERSATION.

EXERCISE 3

Practice the conversation a few more times with your partner. Each time, use the activities below for inviting and refusing the invitation.

VOCABULARY
- *do homework*
- *do housework*
- *eat out*
- *go shopping*
- *go to the library*
- *watch a video*

UNIT 13

LISTENING TASK

EXERCISE 1

Circle all the things that Zachary invites Mia to do.

EXERCISE 2

Listen again, and make an "X" on the invitations that
she refuses, and check (√) the one that she accepts.

EXERCISE 3

Listen once more and draw a square around each *reason*
that Mia gives Zachary when she refuses, and match the
reason with the invitation.

PAIR WORK   *Do Exercise 1 alone and Exercise 2 with a partner.*

EXERCISE 1

Write the numbers of any sixteen of the activities (1 through 24) in any order on your grid below.

Memo
• DO NOT SHOW YOUR GRID TO YOUR PARTNER.

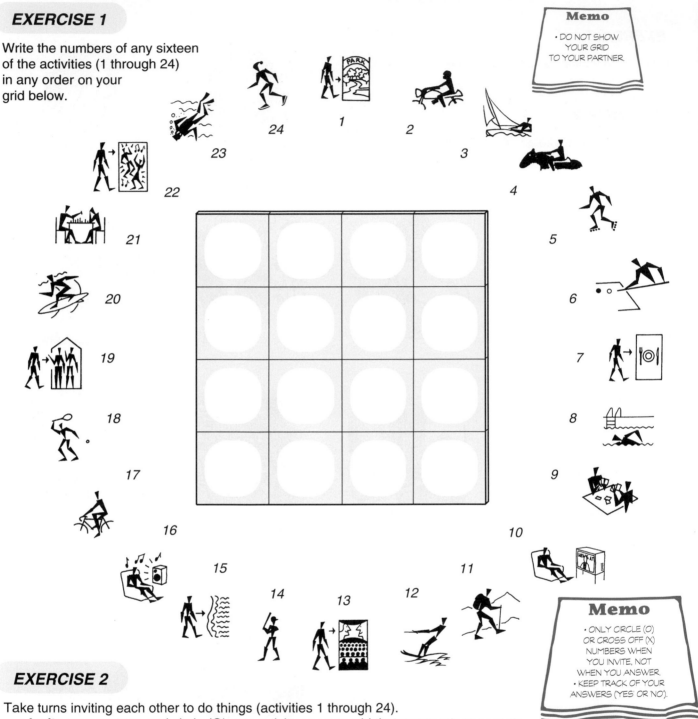

EXERCISE 2

Take turns inviting each other to do things (activities 1 through 24).
- **Invite** your partner, and circle (**O**) any activity on your grid that your partner accepts, and cross off (**X**) any activity on your grid that your partner refuses.
- When you **answer**, you can **accept** or **refuse** any invitation, but <u>you must give a reason if you refuse</u>.

Memo
• ONLY CIRCLE (O) OR CROSS OFF (X) NUMBERS WHEN YOU INVITE, NOT WHEN YOU ANSWER.
• KEEP TRACK OF YOUR ANSWERS (YES' OR NO).

Continue until all your numbers are marked. Each time you get four **O**'s or four **X**'s in a line, shout *"Bingo!"* *The student with the most "bingos" is the winner!*

Examples:

Student A: *Would you like to go to the park on Friday?*
Student B: *Sure, I'd love to.*

Student B: *How about playing tennis on Sunday?*
Student A: *I'm sorry, but I have to work on Sunday.*

GROUP WORK

Do Exercise 1 alone and Exercise 2 with everyone.

EXERCISE 1

Fill in any five mornings, five afternoons, and five evenings on the schedule below with different activities—things that you have to do or dates that you have. (Choose from the activities on the right, or make up your own.)

	Monday	Tuesday	Wednesday	Thursday	Friday	Saturday	Sunday
Morning							
Afternoon							
Evening							

EXERCISE 2

Walk around the classroom and make dates with four different people:
- one person in the morning
- one person in the afternoon
- one person in the evening
- one person anytime

You can only make a date for a time you are free.

For each date that you make (or accept), write on your schedule:
- who you will meet
- the activity (choose from the left, or make up your own)
- what time you will meet
- where you will meet

Memo

- GIVE A REASON EACH TIME YOU REFUSE AN INVITATION.
- IF SOMEONE REFUSES YOUR INVITATION, SUGGEST ANOTHER TIME.

Example:

Student A: *Would you like to go to a movie Friday night?*
Student B: *I'm sorry, but I have to work.*
Student A: *Then how about Saturday night?*
Student B: *Sure, that sounds great.*
Student A: *Okay, how about meeting at my house around six?*
Student B: *Sure, that's fine.*

14 IT'S GONNA RAIN

WARM-UP EXERCISES

EXERCISE 1

Write one or two sentences in the empty speech balloon.

You're going to meet a woman with blonde hair...

EXERCISE 2

Practice the following conversation with *two* other students. (Take turns as *Ron, Dan,* and *Judy.*)

Ron:	I'm sure the Yankees will win.
Dan:	Yeah, they're definitely going to win!
Judy:	I don't know. Maybe they'll win.
(Later)	
Ron:	The Yankees are definitely going to lose.
Dan:	Yeah, they're going to lose.
Judy:	I'm not sure. They might lose.

EXERCISE 3

Practice the conversation a few more times with the other students. Each time, use one idea below to make different predictions.

Memo

• ALWAYS LOOK AT THE PERSON YOU ARE SPEAKING TO—DON'T LOOK DOWN AT THE TEXT!
• YOU CAN ALSO MAKE PREDICTIONS ABOUT OTHER THINGS.

LISTENING TASK

EXERCISE 1

Listen to the conversation and circle any picture that represents a prediction that you hear.

EXERCISE 2

Listen to the conversation again. Next to each of the predictions, write a "√ " if the person is certain, and a "?" if the person isn't sure.

EXERCISE 3

Listen once more and make a note of each prediction.

PAIR WORK

Student A:

Look at each question on page 71 and
make a prediction about *Student B's* future.
- If *Student B* agrees, check (√) *"Agrees."*
- If *Student B* disagrees, check (√) *"Disagrees."*

Student B:

Listen to *Student A's* predictions and tell
Student A if you agree or disagree.

	Agrees	Disagrees
Examples:		
Student A: *I think you will definitely be a student at this school next year.*	✓	☐
Student B: *Your'e right, I will.*		
Student A: *I think you might be a student. at this school next year.*	☐	✓
Student B: *No, I don't think so.*		
Student A: *I don't think you'll be a student. at this school next year.*	✓	☐
Student B: *I don't think so either.*		

Memo
• STUDENT B: CLOSE
YOUR BOOK AND ANSWER
TRUTHFULLY.
• DO THIS EXERCISE
AGAIN–TAKE TURNS
AS <u>STUDENT A</u> AND
<u>STUDENT B</u>.

Do you think your partner will...

	Agrees	Disagrees
...be a student at this school next year?	☐	☐
...study another foreign language besides English someday?	☐	☐
...go overseas to study someday?	☐	☐
...change jobs some time during the next five years?	☐	☐
...be living in the same place two years from now?	☐	☐
...buy a car this year?	☐	☐
...buy a house some time during the next ten years?	☐	☐
...have grandchildren someday?	☐	☐
...go abroad on vacation in the next few years?	☐	☐
...live in another country some time in the future?	☐	☐
...be famous someday?	☐	☐
...(Write and ask your own question:) ....?	☐	☐

Total: _ _ _ _ _ _   _ _ _ _ _ _

GROUP WORK
Do Exercise 1 with your group and Exercise 2 with everyone.

EXERCISE 1

- In your group, discuss some predictions about both the near future and the distant future. (See the *topic box* for ideas, or use your own ideas.) You are going to tell the other students in the class one prediction about news about the near future (a), and one about life in the distant future (b).

- Work out different predictions for each member of your group, and write your own two predictions in the boxes below.

TOPIC BOX

(a) News about the near future:
- *the weather*
- *sports news*
- *a famous person in the news*

(b) Life in the distant future:
- *at home*
- *at school*
- *at work*

Prediction (a)	**Prediction (b)**
....	....
....	....
....	....

Memo

· MAKE PREDICTIONS IN DIFFERENT WAYS, USING "GOING TO", "WILL", "MAYBE", "MIGHT", ETC.

EXERCISE 2

Go around the classroom and tell your predictions to the other students in the class.
Make a check (√) in a box below for the response to each prediction *("Agrees" or "Disagrees")*.

(a)		(b)	
Agrees	**Disagrees**	**Agrees**	**Disagrees**

Also, agree or disagree with other students' predictions—and if you *disagree,* give your own opinion.

Examples:

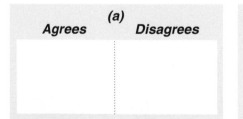

Student A: *I think the Knicks are going to win tonight!*
Student B: *I think so, too.*

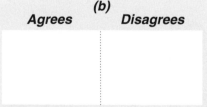

Student C: *We'll probably <u>fly</u> everywhere in 100 years.*
Student D: *I don't think so. I think we'll still use cars.*

SAY THAT AGAIN

WARM-UP EXERCISES

Do Exercise 1 alone and Exercise 2 with a partner.

EXERCISE 1

Below are four different conversations, and each conversation has four sentences (boxes 1 through 4).
Match the sentences on the left and right to make each conversation (*1, 2, 3,* and *4*).

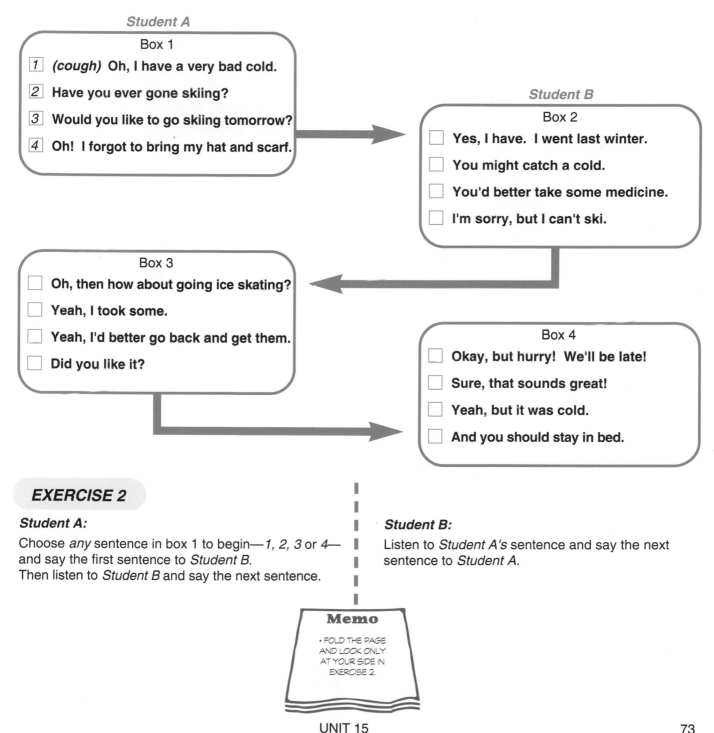

Student A

Box 1

1. *(cough)* Oh, I have a very bad cold.
2. Have you ever gone skiing?
3. Would you like to go skiing tomorrow?
4. Oh! I forgot to bring my hat and scarf.

Student B

Box 2

☐ Yes, I have. I went last winter.
☐ You might catch a cold.
☐ You'd better take some medicine.
☐ I'm sorry, but I can't ski.

Box 3

☐ Oh, then how about going ice skating?
☐ Yeah, I took some.
☐ Yeah, I'd better go back and get them.
☐ Did you like it?

Box 4

☐ Okay, but hurry! We'll be late!
☐ Sure, that sounds great!
☐ Yeah, but it was cold.
☐ And you should stay in bed.

EXERCISE 2

Student A:

Choose *any* sentence in box 1 to begin—*1, 2, 3* or *4*—
and say the first sentence to *Student B*.
Then listen to *Student B* and say the next sentence.

Student B:

Listen to *Student A's* sentence and say the next
sentence to *Student A*.

Memo

• FOLD THE PAGE
AND LOOK ONLY
AT YOUR SIDE IN
EXERCISE 2.

LISTENING TASK

EXERCISE 1

Listen to the conversations (1 through 5) and write the number
of each conversation on the correct picture.

EXERCISE 2

Listen again and write the *key words* next to each picture.

Memo
• KEY WORDS ARE
IMPORTANT WORDS,
OR WORDS
THAT TELL YOU
WHICH PICTURE TO
CHOOSE.

PAIR WORK

EXERCISE 1

Give *Student B* clues for each answer in *CROSSWORD PUZZLE 1*
until *Student B* guesses the answer. Use "blanks" in your clues.
(You can give more than one clue for an answer.)

Memo

• FOR HELP MAKING
CLUES, YOU CAN LOOK AT
THE UNIT SHOWN FOR
EACH WORD, BUT TRY
TO MAKE UP YOUR
OWN SENTENCES.

Example:

Student B: What's 1 down?
Student A: I "blank" with you—I don't think cats are smarter than dogs.
Student B: Disagree?
Student A: That's right!

CROSSWORD PUZZLE 1

Unit 8   Warm-up   Unit 12   Unit 6   Unit 8   Unit 13

¹D A N G ²E R ³O U ⁴S   Unit 9
 I   V   K   U
 S   ⁵G E   A   R
⁶T A K E R   Y   E   Unit 4
 G   R   ⁷T
⁸R E M E M B E R   U   Unit 7
 E   A   U
 E   N   ⁹L O V E   Unit 13

Unit 4-Instructions

Unit 13-Inviting

Unit 7-Excuses & Reasons

Unit 12-Experiences

Warm-Up-Personal Information

Unit 8-Opinions

Unit 9-Comparisons

Unit 6-Permission

EXERCISE 2

Ask *Student B* for clues and fill in *CROSSWORD PUZZLE 2*.
In each clue, the "blank" in *Student B's* sentence is the answer.

Example:

Student A: What's 1 down?
Student B: He's poor now, but I'm sure he'll be rich "blank".
Student A: Someday?
Student B: That's right!

CROSSWORD PUZZLE 2

GROUP WORK   *Do this exercise in groups of three or four.*

Student A:

Tell the group a story about yourself. *The story must be 100% true or 100% false.*
Don't tell the other students in your group if it is true or false—they will ask you
questions about your story, and then tell you whether they think it is true or false.

Students B, C, & D:

- Listen to *Student A's* story and then ask questions about the story.
- Afterwards tell *Student A* whether you think the story is true or false.

Memo

• EACH STUDENT
TAKE A TURN
AS <u>STUDENT A</u> AND
TELL THE GROUP
A STORY.

LANGUAGE GAME

Play this game with two to four "players" and one "caller".

Player

CALLER:
LOOK AT
PAGE 90

Take turns choosing two numbers (1 through 20) from the grid below.
Each number is a question or an answer. The caller will read each sentence that you choose.
Choose one number, listen to the caller read the sentence, and then choose another number.
Try to match a question with the answer.

Do not write any notes—*just listen!*

①	②	③	④	⑤
⑥	⑦	⑧	⑨	⑩
⑪	⑫	⑬	⑭	⑮
⑯	⑰	⑱	⑲	⑳

Continue until all the questions and answers have been matched.
The player with the most matches is the *winner!*

Memo
• CHECK (√) THE NUMBERS THAT <u>YOU</u> MATCH.
• CROSS OFF (X) THE NUMBERS THAT <u>ANOTHER PLAYER</u> MATCHES.
• LOOK AT THIS PAGE <u>ONLY</u>!

STUDENT B PAGES

PAIR WORK

Warm-Up Unit

EXERCISE 1

Take turns with *Student A* asking and answering questions about the three people, and fill in the blanks in the boxes (1 through 3).

Memo
- USE "SHE", "HE", AND "THEY" IN YOUR QUESTIONS AND ANSWERS (IN BOXES 1-3).

Example:

Student A: *Where does Jenny live?*
Student B: *She lives in Malibu.*

1

I'm a _____ and I live in Malibu. I can speak Spanish and a little Greek. I _____ in my spare time.

Jenny

2

I live in _____ and I'm a journalist. I can speak _____. My hobby is mountain-climbing.

Phil

3

We live in London. We are both teachers, and both of us can speak _____ _____. In our free time we _____.

Harry and Lisa

4

Student A

_____
name

EXERCISE 2

Take turns with *Student A* asking and answering the same questions about each other for box 4. Then write a paragraph about *Student A* in box 4.

Use "you" in your questions, and "he" or "she" in your paragraph.

PAIR WORK

Unit 1

EXERCISE 1

You work at the Port Authority Bus Terminal.
Look at the bus schedule and answer
Student A's questions.

PORT AUTHORITY BUS TERMINAL BUS INFORMATION		
DESTINATION:	*MIAMI*	*DENVER*
FARE:	*$102*	*$119*
	Departs Arrives	Departs Arrives
DAILY DEPARTURE AND ARRIVAL TIMES:	6:00 6:15	6:15 4:45
	8:30 8:45	8:40 7:10
	10:40 10:55	10:50 9:20
	13:30 13:45	13:40 12:10
	15:30 15:45	15:30 14:00
	16:30 16:45	17:00 15:30
	17:45 18:00	18:00 16:30
	19:00 19:15	22:00 20:30
ARRIVAL DAY:	*+ one day*	*+ two days*
TRAVEL TIME:	*24 hrs. 15 min.*	*48 hrs. 30 min.*

EXERCISE 2

1. You are going to take a train trip from New York City to *Chicago* or *L.A.*
Choose *which city* you want to go and *when* you want to leave.
Write the information in the blanks below before you speak to *Student A*:

I'd like to go to _____ on _____
              city   day
at about _____ o'clock in the _____ .
        time   time of day

2. *Student A* works at New York Penn Station. Ask *Student A* for
information and write the answers on the memo pad on the right.

Example:

Student A: *Can I help you?*
Student B: *Yes, I'd like to go to Chicago on Tuesday at about 3 o'clock*
in the afternoon.
Student A: *Okay, we have trains around that time.*
Student B: *Great! Could you tell me . . .?*

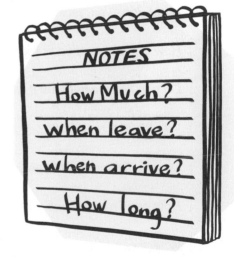

NOTES

How Much?

when leave?

when arrive?

How long?

EXERCISE 3

INTERNATIONAL LANGUAGE SCHOOL

Memo
• DO EXERCISE 3
AGAIN–TAKE TURNS
AS <u>STUDENT A</u> AND
<u>STUDENT B</u>.

You want to take a language course this summer.
Student A is a language school manager.
Choose a language to study and ask *Student A* for information.
Make a note of your questions and the answers.
(See the box below for ideas.)

Example:

Student B: *Could you tell me if you have a Chinese course?*
Student A: *Yes, we do.*
Student B: *Okay, could you tell me . . .?*

POSSIBLE THINGS TO ASK ABOUT		
• _____language	• *Course dates*	• *Class times*
• *Placement test*	• *Length of course*	• *Students*
• *Teachers*	• *Costs*	• *School location*

LANGUAGE GAME

Unit 5

Play this game with two to four "players" and one "caller".

1. Number the questions and answers below from 1 to 24 in *random order* (i.e., all mixed up).

2. The players will take turns choosing pairs of numbers.
   When you hear the first number, read the first sentence.
   When you hear the second number, read the second sentence.
   • If the two sentences *match,* say "Match!" and write the player's name next to the sentences.
     After that, the next player chooses.
   • If the two sentences *do not match,* say "No match."
     After that, the next player chooses.

Question:	*Answer:*	*Player's name:*
◯ Could you lend me your pen?	◯ Of course—here you are.	....
◯ Could you tell me how long the trip is?	◯ It takes about 48 hours.	....
◯ What does your jacket look like?	◯ Well, it's plaid and it has black buttons.	....
◯ How do you use this ticket machine?	◯ Put in the money and press this button.	....
◯ Do you know what time it leaves?	◯ Every hour on the hour.	....
◯ What is that made of?	◯ Mostly glass, but this part is plastic.	....
◯ Do you think you could give me a ride?	◯ Sure, no problem—it's on my way home.	....
◯ How can I make a call on this phone?	◯ First dial "9", and then the phone number.	....
◯ Where can I cash traveller's checks?	◯ There's a bank around the corner.	....
◯ Do you know how to close this?	◯ Yeah, just turn it clockwise.	....
◯ Would you mind calling me back later?	◯ Not at all—I'll call around five o'clock.	....
◯ Is it big?	◯ No, it's small enough to fit in your pocket.	....

Continue until all the questions and answers are matched.
The player with the most matches is the *winner!*

Play again—each student take a turn as the caller.

Memo
• READ EACH SENTENCE
  SLOWLY, ONCE
  OR TWICE.
• READ <u>BOTH</u> OF THE
SENTENCES, AND THEN SAY
"MATCH" OR "NO MATCH".

STUDENT B

PAIR WORK

Unit 6

EXERCISE 1

You are a college student.
Student A is your roommate.
Look at the information in the box.
Answer *Student A's* requests.
(You can give or refuse permission.)

Example:

Student B: *Is it okay if I come to work an hour late on Monday?*

Student A: *I'm sorry, but . . .*

Student A is a great roommate. You usually say "Yes" to *Student A's* requests, but remember these things:

• You are going to take a friend to a drive-in movie Friday night.
• You have to watch a documentary on TV tonight for history class.
• You are going to take pictures at a friend's wedding on Sunday.

EXERCISE 2

You are an office worker. *Student A* is your boss.
Ask *Student A* for permission to:

Check (√):
*Permission
given refused*

• take a thirty-minute break to go to the bank.

• take this Friday off.

• come to work an hour late on Monday.

• take a two-hour lunch break tomorrow.

• make a personal overseas phone call.

• use the company car over the weekend.

• get a new telephone.

• take a four-week vacation this summer.

EXERCISE 3

You are a teacher.
Student A is your student
Look at the information in the box.
Answer *Student A's* requests.
(You can give or refuse permission.)

Student A is a good student. You usually say "Yes" to *Student A's* requests, but remember these things:

• You do not like it when students come to class late.
• You do not let students leave early unless it's an emergency.
• You do not want *Student A* to miss any classes.

EXERCISE 4

You are a teenager. *Student A* is your parent
(mother/father). Ask *Student A* if you can:

Check (√):
*Permission
given refused*

invite a friend to dinner.

get a part-time job in the evening.

go on a camping trip with friends.

buy a small motorcycle.

sleep at a friend's house this weekend.

paint your bedroom black and white.

have a party next weekend.

go to France for the summer with friends.

PAIR WORK

Unit 7

EXERCISE 1

You are a student. *Student A* is your teacher.
Listen to each question and give *Student A* an excuse.
(Use *"I couldn't..."* or *"I had to..."* with the cues below.)

Example:

Student A: *Why didn't you finish the test yesterday?*
Student B: *I couldn't remember the answers.*

- ...remember the answers.
- ...visit my aunt in the hospital.
- ...open my locker.
- ...go to the dentist this morning.
- ...*(make up your own excuse)*
- ...*(make up your own excuse)*

EXERCISE 2

You are *Student A's* mother/father. *Student A* is a teenager.
Ask *Student A* questions. Write down *Student A's* excuses.

Student A didn't...	Student A's excuse:
• clean the basement.	
• do the laundry.	
• take out the garbage.	
• feed the dog.	
• wash the dishes.	
• get a haircut.	

EXERCISE 3

You did not do any of the six things below (1 through 6).
- Write down a reason for each thing you didn't do (1 through 6).
- Walk around the classroom and ask for and give reasons for each one (1 through 6).
  Write down the name of one person who has a *similar* reason next to each one.

You didn't...	Your reason:	
1. go bowling Friday night.		name
2. go swimming on Saturday.		name
3. go to the big party Saturday night.		name
4. play ball Sunday morning.		name
5. go shopping on Sunday.		name
6. go to the movies Sunday night.		name

PAIR WORK

Unit 10

EXERCISE 1

Write a comparison for each picture (1 through 4):   Write a request for permission for each picture (5 through 8):

1	
2	
3	
4	

5	
6	
7	
8	

EXERCISE 2

Take turns with *Student A* guessing what each other wrote for each picture in *Exercise 1*.
These are *Student A's* pictures from *Exercise 1*:

Comparisons   *Requests for permission*

Memo
• EACH STUDENT
CAN MAKE ONLY
ONE GUESS PER TURN.
• THE WORDING DOES
NOT HAVE TO BE
EXACTLY THE SAME.

*The first one to guess
all eight correctly
is the winner!*

Examples:

Student A: *Did you write, "A plane
is faster than a bus"?*

Student B: *No, I didn't.*

Student B: *Did you write, "The man is
shorter than the woman"?*

Student A: *Yes, I did.*

PAIR WORK

Unit 10

Memo
• USE DIFFERENT
  EXPRESSIONS
  TO AGREE
  OR DISAGREE.

EXERCISE 3

Listen to *Student A's* opinions. Use one of the replies below to agree or disagree with *Student A.*

○ (AGREE) + "I like to stay in one place and relax."

○ (DISAGREE) + "It's one of the most important events in your life."

○ (DISAGREE) + "I think both are very difficult for non-native speakers."

○ (AGREE) + "Last night I saw six murders in one hour!"

○ (AGREE) + "Some people lose their life savings!"

EXERCISE 4

Tell *Student A* your opinions (1 through 5) and write down *Student A's* reply to each one.

1 Student B: *In my opinion, everyone should have a computer these days.*
   Student A: ....

2 Student B: *I think professional athletes' salaries are much too high. They're overpaid.*
   Student A: ....

3 Student B: *I believe real school classrooms are much better than internet classes.*
   Student A: ....

4 Student B: *I don't care what they say—I don't think airplanes are safe.*
   Student A: ....

5 Student B: *I think this pair work exercise is really interesting, don't you?*
   Student A: ....

EXERCISE 5

Discuss all the topics with your partner, giving your <u>own</u> opinions.

LANGUAGE GAME

Play this game with two to four "players" and one "caller".

Caller

PLAYER:
LOOK AT
PAGE 54

Unit 10

1. Number the questions and answers below from 1 to 24 in *random order* (i.e., all mixed up).

2. The players will take turns choosing pairs of numbers.
When you hear the first number, read the first sentence.
When you hear the second number, read the second sentence.
• If the two sentences *match,* say "Match!" and write the player's name next to the sentences.
  After that, the next player chooses.
• If the two sentences *do not match,* say "No match."
  After that, the next player chooses.

Question:	Answer:	Player's name:
◯ Can I use your calculator for a minute?	◯ Of course—it's on the table over there.	....
◯ Why didn't you hand in the homework?	◯ I'm sorry, but my cat tore it up.	....
◯ What do you think of life in New York?	◯ It can be dangerous, but I love it!	....
◯ Is this house larger than yours?	◯ Actually, I think it's smaller.	....
◯ Mind if I turn off the TV?	◯ Not at all—go ahead.	....
◯ Why didn't you clean your room?	◯ Well, I couldn't find the vacuum cleaner.	....
◯ The new mayor is great, isn't he?	◯ Actually, I'm not sure about him.	....
◯ Is the Nile longer than the Mississippi?	◯ Sure, it's about 1800 miles longer.	....
◯ Could I possibly use your car tonight?	◯ I'm sorry, but it has two flat tires.	....
◯ Why weren't you at my surprise party?	◯ I wasn't invited!	....
◯ I think TV is bad for children, don't you?	◯ Well, I think that too much can be harmful.	....
◯ Is your dog friendlier than your cat?	◯ Yeah, but my cat is smarter.	....

Continue until all the questions and answers are matched.
The player with the most matches is the *winner!*

Play again—each student take a turn as the caller.

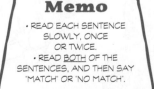

Memo
• READ EACH SENTENCE
SLOWLY, ONCE
OR TWICE.
• READ <u>BOTH</u> OF THE
SENTENCES, AND THEN SAY
"MATCH" OR "NO MATCH".

STUDENT B

PAIR WORK

Unit 11

EXERCISE 1

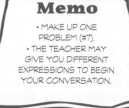

Memo
• MAKE UP ONE
PROBLEM (#7).
• THE TEACHER MAY
GIVE YOU DIFFERENT
EXPRESSIONS TO BEGIN
YOUR CONVERSATION.

You have a problem.
- Tell *Student A* your problems (1 through 7).
  (Begin by saying something like "Oh no!" or "Ohhh....")
- Write down *Student A's* advice below each problem.

1. You lost your ATM card.

2. You have stomach pain and a fever.

3. You have a big test on Monday.

4. Someone stole your bicycle!

5. You have a headache.

6. You left your wallet at a restaurant.

7. *(make up a problem)*

EXERCISE 2

Memo
• GIVE ADVICE
IN DIFFERENT WAYS.
• MAKE UP
YOUR OWN ADVICE
FOR ONE PROBLEM.

Student A has a problem.
- Listen and ask *Student A*: "What's wrong?" or "What's the matter?"
- Listen to *Student A's* problems and give *Student A* advice.

Choose advice to give *Student A* from the pictures below.

Example:

Student A: *Ohhh...!*
Student B: *What's wrong?*
Student A: *I left my camera on the train!*
Student B: *Why don't you go to the "Lost and Found" office?*

(Make up your own advice)

PAIR WORK

Unit 11

EXERCISE 3

You are taking a trip to Hong Kong.
- Tell *Student A* your plans (1 through 5).
- Ask *Student A* for advice and write it down.

Example:

Student B: *I'm going to stay at the Excelsior Hotel.
Do you think that's a good idea?*
Student A: *Why don't you stay at the YMCA?
It's much cheaper.*

1. ...stay at the Excelsior Hotel.

2. ...travel around Hong Kong by taxi.

3. ...take cash to go shopping.

4. ...go sightseeing alone.

5. ...*(make up a plan)*

EXERCISE 4

First, tell *Student A* the name of a place that you know well.
Then give *Student A* advice about where to stay, what to see,
how to get around, etc., in that place.

Memo

• DO EXERCISE 4
TWICE–TAKE TURNS
AS STUDENT A AND
STUDENT B.

Example:

Student B: *I grew up in Singapore.*
Student A: *Oh, really? I'm going there on
vacation next summer! Listen,
could you tell me...*

PAIR WORK

Unit 12

STUDENT A: LOOK AT PAGE 62

Take turns with *Student A* asking and answering questions about the people below. For the empty boxes, find out:
- *where* they have been (ask about places in the box below)
- *when* they went there
- *why* they went

Memo
- DO NOT READ THE SENTENCES TO STUDENT A—JUST ANSWER THE QUESTIONS!

PLACES		
• Colorado	• Australia	• Spain
• Florida	• Vienna	• Israel

First write *notes* of the answers *next* to each empty box, and later write one sentence with all the information *in* each box.

Example:

Student A: Has Kurt ever been to Hong Kong?

Student B: No, he hasn't.

(Afterwards compare sentences with your partner.)

Jim

Emilio

Katrina

Ten years ago Katrina flew to Moscow to visit her brother, and she met her brother's wife and children for the first time.

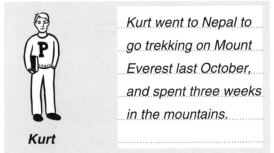

Kurt

Kurt went to Nepal to go trekking on Mount Everest last October, and spent three weeks in the mountains.

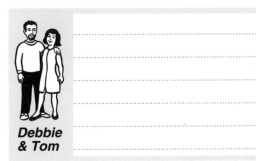

Debbie & Tom

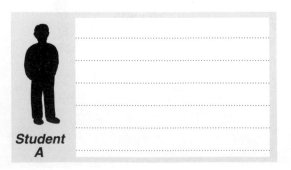

Student A

Jack & Eri

During the winter vacation Jack and Eri travelled to Hong Kong to go shopping, and they spent a lot of money.

PAIR WORK

Unit 15

EXERCISE 1

Ask *Student A* for clues and fill in *CROSSWORD PUZZLE 1*.
In each clue, the "blank" in *Student A's* sentence is the answer.

Example:

Student B: *What's 1 down?*
Student A: *I "blank" with you—I don't think cats are smarter than dogs.*
Student B: *Disagree?*
Student A: *That's right!*

CROSSWORD PUZZLE 1

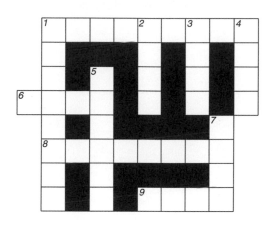

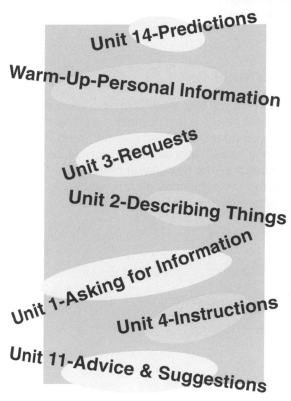

Unit 14-Predictions

Warm-Up-Personal Information

Unit 3-Requests

Unit 2-Describing Things

Unit 1-Asking for Information

Unit 4-Instructions

Unit 11-Advice & Suggestions

EXERCISE 2

Give *Student A* clues for each answer in
CROSSWORD PUZZLE 2 until *Student A*
guesses the answer. Use "blanks" in your clues.
(You can give more than one clue for an answer.)

Example:

Student A: *What's 1 down?*
Student B: *He's poor now, but I'm sure he'll be rich "blank".*
Student A: *Someday?*
Student B: *That's right!*

CROSSWORD PUZZLE 2

Unit 14   Unit 2   Unit 11   Unit 1   Unit 3

Unit 3
Unit 4
Warm-up
Unit 11
Unit 14

Memo
• FOR HELP MAKING
CLUES, YOU CAN LOOK AT
THE UNIT SHOWN FOR
EACH WORD, BUT TRY
TO MAKE UP YOUR
OWN SENTENCES.

LANGUAGE GAME

Unit 15

Play this game with two to four "players" and one "caller".

Caller

PLAYER:
LOOK AT
PAGE 77

EXERCISE 1

Look through the book for ideas and write ten questions and answers side by side in the blanks below.
Then number the questions and answers from 1 to 20 in *random order* (i.e., all mixed up).

Memo
· EXERCISE 1
MAY BE ASSIGNED
AS HOMEWORK.
· DO EXERCISE 1
ALONE.

EXERCISE 2

The players will take turns choosing pairs of numbers.
When you hear the first number, read the first sentence.
When you hear the second number, read the second sentence.
- If the two sentences *match,* say "Match!" and write the player's name next to the sentences.
  After that, the next player chooses.
- If the two sentences *do not match,* say "No match."
  After that, the next player chooses.

Question: *Answer:*   *Player's name:*

Continue until all the questions and answers are matched.
The player with the most matches is the *winner!*

Play again—each student take a turn as the caller.

Memo
· IMPORTANT:
MAKE SURE THAT EACH
ANSWER CANNOT BE USED
WITH ANY OTHER QUESTION.
· THE TEACHER SHOULD
CHECK YOUR SENTENCES
BEFORE EXERCISE 2.

90   STUDENT B

HOMEWORK PAGES

HOMEWORK

EXERCISE 1

In each of the situations below, one person is getting information from another person. Write a question and answer for each of the situations (1 through 6).

Memo
• WRITE A DIFFERENT QUESTION AND ANSWER FOR EACH SITUATION.

BANK

1

2

IMMIGRATION

AIRPORT

3

4

PET STORE

TRAVEL AGENCY

5

6

TRAIN STATION

EXERCISE 2   *(OPTIONAL)*

In class, the teacher will have you write only one of your questions (1 through 6) on the board, along with the other students.
Then look at the other questons on the board and write any of your answers (1 through 6) below any questions that they match.

Memo
• DO EXERCISE 2 IN THE NEXT LESSON IF YOU HAVE TIME.
• DO NOT WRITE THE ANSWER TO <u>YOUR OWN</u> QUESTION ON THE BOARD.

Examples (written on board):

Student A's *question:*   Do you know what time the bank opens?
Student B's *answer:*   It opens at 9 a.m.

Student B's *question:*   Could you tell me the flight number?
Student C's *answer:*   It's Flight 351.

HOMEWORK

EXERCISE 1

Find a large picture of an interesting object in a magazine or newspaper.
Cut out the picture and bring it to class.
Write a complete description of the object on the lines below.
(Write three or more sentences.)

Memo
• BRING A LARGE
PICTURE OF
ONLY <u>ONE</u> OBJECT.
• MAKE SURE THE
PICTURE IS BIG ENOUGH
FOR THE WHOLE CLASS
TO SEE FROM THE BOARD.

Examples:

- It's large and square.
- It's made of plastic, glass and metal.
- It has speakers and a microphone.

EXERCISE 2   *(OPTIONAL)*

In class, work in a group of three or four students.
The teacher will put everyone's picture on the board and number each picture.

Student A: Choose <u>any</u> picture on the board. *(It does not have to be your picture.)*
Answer questions ("yes," "no," or "partly") until someone guesses the picture.

Students B, C, D: Take turns asking *Student A* "yes/no" questions about the
objects on the board until you can guess the correct picture.

Memo
• DO EXERCISE 2
IN THE NEXT LESSON
IF YOU HAVE TIME.
• ALL QUESTIONS MUST BE
ABOUT <u>DESCRIPTIONS</u>.

Example:

Student B: Is it made of plastic?
Student A: Partly.
Student C: Is it round?
Student A: No, it isn't.
Student D: Does it have speakers and a microphone?
Student B: Yes, it does.
Student D: Is it picture number five?
Student B: Yes!

HOMEWORK

EXERCISE 1

Match the pictures with the dialogs and write a request in each of the dialogs.

1

Stella:	_____?
Lisa:	I'm in the kitchen and my hands are full right now, Stella. Can you get it?
Stella:	Oh, all right—but it's probably for you.

2

Professor Hall:	Yes, Ann-Marie, what is it?
Ann-Marie:	_____?
Professor Hall:	Of course. Come by between three and five.
Ann-Marie:	Great, thank you. I'll be there at 3:30.

3

Jack:	I'm going to the store, Jill. Need anything?
Jill:	_____?
Jack:	What kind do you want?
Jill:	Oh, it doesn't matter—just get the largest they have.

4

Mom:	_____?
Tommy:	But I just walked him an hour ago!
Mom:	That was more like *three* hours ago—and anyway, he wants to go out.
Tommy:	Oh, okay. Come on, Socrates.

EXERCISE 2

Draw a simple sketch and write a short dialog with a request.

HOMEWORK

EXERCISE 1

Unscramble the instructions below. Then write each line below the correct New York subway sign (1 through 6).

- *instructions from listen crew for*
- *lean do doors on not*
- *stay car in*
- *cars not ride do between*
- *pull brake do emergency not*
- *onto straps hand hold*

IN AN EMERGENCY:

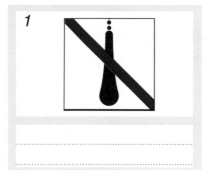

1

2

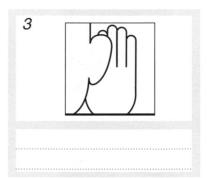

3

WHILE TRAIN IS MOVING:

4

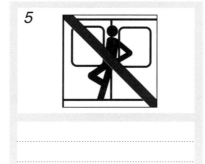

5

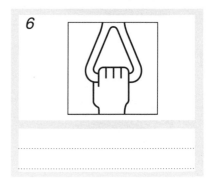

6

EXERCISE 2

Write instructions for each subway sign.

AT ALL TIMES:

1

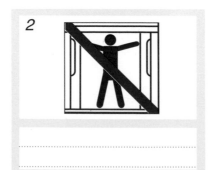

2

3

(Draw your own sign:)

HOMEWORK

EXERCISE 1

Match the pictures with the dialogs and write a request for permission in each of the dialogs.

1
Rob:	.... ?
Deb:	No, go right ahead, Rob.
Rob:	Thanks. I'll open a window so it won't bother you.
Deb:	No, that's okay—don't worry about it.

2
Tommy:	.... ?
Dad:	Where to, Tommy?
Tommy:	To my pen pal in Japan. I want to say "Happy birthday."
Dad:	Well, okay, but don't talk too long.

3
René:	.... ?
Ali:	Sure, René. You can use it all day.
René:	Thanks, but I just need it for a minute. I have one in my locker.
Ali:	Oh, okay.

4
Harold:	.... ?
Sonny:	Sunday? Where do you want to go?
Harold:	I'd like to take Rebecca for a ride in the mountains.
Sonny:	Okay, but be careful, Harold.

EXERCISE 2

Draw a simple sketch and write a short dialog with a request for permission and an answer.

HOMEWORK

EXERCISE 1

Look at the thoughts of each person that didn't go to Mike's party
and write a reason for each person on a separate sheet of paper.

EXERCISE 2 (OPTIONAL)

In class, practice the exchanges with a partner.
Take turns asking and answering the question:
"Why didn't you go to Mike's party?"

Memo
- DO EXERCISE 2
IN THE NEXT LESSON
IF YOU HAVE TIME.
- DO NOT LOOK AT
YOUR BOOK WHEN
ANSWERING THE QUESTION.

HOMEWORK

EXERCISE 1

For each opinion below (1 through 6), write one reply.
Agree and give a reason (in column 1),
or disagree and give a reason (in column 2).

Memo
• USE DIFFERENT
EXPRESSIONS WHEN YOU
AGREE OR DISAGREE.
• FOR EACH ONE, WRITE
IN COLUMN 1 (AGREE)
OR COLUMN 2 (DISAGREE),
BUT NOT BOTH.

OPINION:	1. REPLY: (Agree / reason)	2. REPLY: (Disagree / reason)
1 I don't think teachers should give a lot of homework.		
2 I think all airplanes should have a smoking section.		
3 In my opinion, people should not ride bicycles in the park.		
4 I don't think people should bring baby strollers into the subway.		
5 I think that beaches should not allow people to play music.		
6 I believe that taxis should pick up people with pets.		

EXERCISE 2   (OPTIONAL)

In class, walk around and talk to different partners. Take turns
giving opinions (1 through 6) and replying (agreeing or disagreeing).
For each opinion, find someone who disagrees with your *written reply,*
and write that person's reply next to yours (in column 1 or 2).

Memo
• USE YOUR WRITTEN
REPLIES TO AGREE OR
DISAGREE WITH OPINIONS
—BUT DON'T LOOK DOWN
WHEN SPEAKING!

HOMEWORK

Write four opinion questions and four factual questions, comparing two things in each question.
See the box below for ideas, or use your own ideas.

IDEAS FOR COMPARISONS

• animals	• cities	• countries	• famous people
• languages	• food	• music	• mountains
• oceans	• rivers	• sports	• TV programs

Examples:

(Opinion questions)
- *Which do you think is more interesting, rock music or jazz?*
- *Do you think soccer is more exciting than baseball?*

(Factual questions)
- *Is the Amazon River longer than the Mississippi River?*
- *Which is larger, Australia or the United States?*

1. ....
2. ....
3. ....
4. ....
5. ....
6. ....
7. ....
8. ....

Memo
- DO EXERCISE 2 IN THE NEXT LESSON IF YOU HAVE TIME.
- MAKE SURE YOU KNOW THE <u>ANSWER</u> TO YOUR OWN FACTUAL QUESTIONS.

EXERCISE 2   *(OPTIONAL)*

In class, walk around and talk to different partners.
Take turns asking and answering the questions (1 through 8).

For each of your *factual* questions, try to find someone who can answer it correctly, and write that person's name next to your question. (If no one can answer it, write "no one.")

HOMEWORK

EXERCISE 1

Look at each couple's thoughts and write a suggestion in each dialog.
(Use *"We should...,"* *"We ought to...,"* or *"Why don't we...?"* for the suggestions.)

1

Husband:	It's our first wedding anniversary next month, honey! What shall we do to celebrate?
Wife:	....
Husband:	Well, it'll be expensive, but okay! Let's go!

2

Husband:	Our third anniversary is just two weeks away! What do you think we should do?
Wife:	....
Husband:	That's a great idea! We can invite everyone!

3

Wife:	Next week's our fifth anniversary. What do you want to do?
Husband:	....
Wife:	Sure, that sounds nice—just the two of us.

4

Wife:	It's our tenth anniversary this Friday. Do you want to do anything?
Husband:	....
Wife:	Yeah, okay—we haven't been out in a while.

5

Wife:	Today's our twentieth anniversary... John? John!
Husband:	....
Wife:	Okay. Is there anything good on?

EXERCISE 2

Draw a simple sketch in the thought balloon and write the rest of the dialog.

Wife:	Tomorrow is our fiftieth anniversary, John. Let's do something.
Husband:	....
Wife:	....

HOMEWORK

EXERCISE 1

Write a *"Have you ever ~ ?"* question for each of the eight pictures.

1. ....

2. ....

3. ....

4. ....

5. ....

6. ....

7. ....

8. *(Make up your own experience)*

EXERCISE 2

Use one of the ideas above, and write a conversation between you and a friend, with your friend asking the questions. Your experience can be *true* or *imaginary*.

Memo

• IN CLASS, PRACTICE YOUR CONVERSATION WITH A PARTNER AS YOUR FRIEND.
• ANSWER YOUR FRIEND'S QUESTIONS WITHOUT LOOKING AT THE TEXT.

Friend: Have you ever .... ?

You: Yes, I have, actually.

Friend: ....

You: ....

Friend: ....

You: ....

Friend: ....

You: ....

HOMEWORK

Write the lines of this dialog *in order* on the lines below.

Well, listen, Rob, would you like to go to a movie Sunday night?

That sounds great—where shall we meet?

A concert? Oh, then maybe another time...

Hi, Diane, it's Rob. How about going to a movie on Saturday afternoon?

Hello?

Sure, six o'clock is fine.

Oh, then how about Saturday night?

I'm sorry, but Saturday night I'm going to a concert with Sue.

That's a great idea.

I'd love to, but I have to work in the afternoon.

How about meeting at the mall around six o'clock?

Good. How about seeing *"The Lost World Revisited"*?

1. Diane:

2. Rob:

3. Diane: *I'd love to, but I have to work in the afternoon.*

4. Rob:

5. Diane:

6. Rob:

7. Diane:

8. Rob: *That's a great idea.*

9. Diane:

10. Rob:

11. Diane: *How about meeting at the mall around six o'clock?*

12. Rob:

EXERCISE 2 (OPTIONAL)

In class, practice the conversation with a partner.
Take turns as *Rob* and *Diane*.
Make sure each line is correct.

Memo

• DO EXERCISE 2 IN THE NEXT LESSON IF YOU HAVE TIME.
• ALWAYS LOOK AT YOUR PARTNER WHEN YOU ARE SPEAKING.

HOMEWORK

101

HOMEWORK

In a hundred years, moon vacations will be very popular.

food   jobs
vacations   the future   health
communication   the future
hobbies   cities
entertainment

Memo
· MAKE PREDICTIONS IN DIFFERENT WAYS, USING "WILL", "MAYBE", "MIGHT", ETC.

EXERCISE 1

Make six predictions about life in the future and write your predictions the lines below.

1. ....
2. ....
3. ....
4. ....
5. ....
6. ....

Memo
· DO EXERCISE 2 IN THE NEXT LESSON IF YOU HAVE TIME.
· YOU CAN ALSO SAY IF YOU AGREE OR DISAGREE WITH EACH PREDICTION YOU HEAR.

EXERCISE 2   *(OPTIONAL)*

In class, walk around and talk to different partners.
Take turns telling each other predictions (1 through 6).
For each of your predictions, try to find someone who made a *similar* prediction, and write that person's name next to your prediction. (If no one made a similar prediction, write "no one.")

TAPESCRIPT

John: Nice party, huh?
Maria: Yeah, it is.
John: Can I get you something to drink?
Maria: Uh, sure, thanks. Just a Coke, please.
John: There you go.
Maria: Thanks.
John: I'm John, by the way, John Fletcher.
Maria: Hi, I'm Maria Gomez. Are you a friend of Jack's?
John: Yeah, we play tennis together.
Maria: Oh, really? So, where are you from?
John: Denver, originally, but I live here in Chicago now. And you?
Maria: Oh, I grew up here in Chicago. I live down the street.
John: So how do you know Jack, Maria?
Maria: We teach at the same school. I'm an art teacher.
John: That's interesting. I'm a graphic designer. Magazine work.
Maria: Really? So you're interested in art...
John: Oh, yeah, very much. I love going to shows.
Maria: Me, too.
John: Oh, yeah? Have you seen the Picasso exhibit at the Art Institute yet?
Maria: No, but—
John: Listen, I'm going tomorrow with Jack and a few friends... Would you like to go with us?
Maria: Sure, I'd love to.
John: And after that, we're all going to the movies—
Maria: Well, okay, that sounds great.
John: Terrific—um, would you like another Coke?
Maria: Oh, well, yeah, but... Is there any diet Coke?

Conversation One
Woman: Sure, Thursday at four is fine. ...Right, okay. Oh, can I ask you one more thing? ...Do you know if I'll be able to eat afterwards? If not, I'll have a late lunch— ...I see, right, I didn't think so, okay, so I'll eat before I come. ...Uh huh, thanks again, bye-bye.

Conversation Two
Woman: Yes, I've looked everywhere—if you don't have it I guess I'll just have to order it. ...Well, do you know how long it'll take if I order it now? ...Two weeks, okay, and do I have to pay for it first, or— ...When I pick it up, I see. ...Okay, I guess I *will* order it now. Could you tell me how much it is, with tax and everything? ...Twenty-one sixty, okay— ...Sure my name is Sally Hill.

Conversation Three
Woman: Four hundred dollars?! I thought it was going to cost about two fifty! ...Yeah I know, but could you tell me what costs so much? ...Uh huh...yeah...I see...okay, well, when will it be ready? ...Seven in the *evening*? ...Okay, Friday at seven—I'll be there. Oh, and, should I call first to make sure it's all done?

Conversation Four
Woman: And could you tell me what time it's over? ...Ten-fifteen, I see, okay, and how much is it? ...Eight fifty, right, okay. Oh, one more thing—do we have to get there early? I mean, do you know if there'll be a long line? ...No? Great, thank you very much.

Conversation One
Clerk: I understand, Miss, but we have a lot of those. Can you tell me what it looks like?
Woman: Well, it's very plain, with almost no design, and it's made of leather—soft brown leather. And it doesn't have a strap or zipper, just one little gold snap. It's a little larger than pocket-size.
Clerk: You lost it this morning?
Woman: That's right, about ten o'clock.
Clerk: Okay, just a minute, I'll see if we have it.

Conversation Two
Girl 1: Yeah, it came this morning—Daddy *told* us he'd send one.
Girl 2: Is it a nice one? What does it look like?
Girl 1: It's mostly black and it has a beautiful design all around it. And it has a nice little silver latch and little silver plates on the corners—it's really beautiful!

Conversation Three
Woman 1: Where did you get that? It looks just like mine!
Woman 2: Really? I bought it in Mexico. Is it exactly the same as yours?
Woman 1: Well, almost. Mine is made of leather, too, and it's the same size, but it has a longer, thinner strap.
Woman 2: Does it have these little leather strings on the front?
Woman 1: Yeah, just like that.

Conversation Four
Boy: What is it, Dad? Come on, tell me!
Dad: Your birthday is *tomorrow*, not today.
Boy: I can't wait! Just tell me what it looks like...please?
Dad: Well, it's small, and it's mostly made of plastic, and it has a little window, and some switches—
Boy: And it has earphones, right?
Dad: Okay, okay, go ahead and open your present.

Conversation Five
Man 1: So, can you buy one for me while you're there?
Man 2: Yeah, sure, but there are so many types. What kind do you want?
Man 1: You know, just a plain brown one, made of *real* leather, of course. I like the ones with two locking latches—key locks, not combination locks.

Conversation Six
Woman: It happened just a minute ago! It was right next to me and now it's gone!
Policeman: Please, ma'am, calm down. What does it look like?
Woman: Well, you know, it's black, and it has a big lens—no case, just a lens cap, and a thin, black shoulder strap. Please hurry, officer! He'll get away!

Larry: It's going to be a great party Saturday night, huh Julie?
Julie: Yeah, but I have a *million* things to do this weekend.
Larry: Is there anything I can do?
Julie: Well, yeah, maybe. Do you think you could take me shopping tonight?
Larry: I guess so.
Julie: Great! Pick me up around six, and—oh yeah! Can you lend me thirty or forty dollars?
Larry: No problem. I have about sixty—
Julie: Sixty is good, Larry, thanks. And later, could you possibly pick up Gina and Marisol and Bonnie and Francine and Maggie?
Larry: Well, it's a small car, but I'd be glad to.
Julie: And listen, I don't have time to do that English homework, so I was wondering if you could possibly write a page or two for me?
Larry: I wish I could, but I really have a lot of homework, and—
Julie: Okay, okay, never mind. But would you mind checking my math homework?
Larry: Not at all. Tonight I have to do *my* math homework, and—
Julie: Are you free tomorrow?
Larry: Tomorrow?
Julie: Yeah. Would it be possible for you to watch my brother Jimmy for an hour or two? I'm supposed to baby-sit after lunch, but—
Larry: I'm afraid I have basketball practice all afternoon, and—
Julie: Basketball practice? But how can I get ready for the party if you can't *do* anything for me?

Exercise One
Conversation One
Woman: Excuse me, Miss? How can I turn on my reading light?
Flight Attendant: Just push this button here, in your armrest—the one with the little light bulb on it.
Woman: Oh yes, I see. Thank you.

Conversation Two
Man: Pardon me, ma'am, but could you tell me how to use these headphones?
Flight Attendant: Sure, just plug them in this hole here...that's right, and push this button to adjust the volume, and turn this dial to change the channel.
Man: Okay, I have it now—thank you very much.

Conversation Three
Flight Attendant: Would you like a blanket or a pillow?
Woman: Not right now, thank you. Maybe later.
Flight Attendant: Okay. If you need to call me for anything, just press this button with the little figure on it.
Woman: Oh, this one next to the light button? Thank you very much.

Conversation Four
Flight Attendant: We're serving dinner now, ma'am. Could you pull your tray down, please?
Woman: Oh yes, um, just a second...
Flight Attendant: First, just turn that lever and then pull the tray down.
Woman: Yes, of course—there.

Conversation Five
Man: Excuse me, how can I adjust my seat?
Flight Attendant: Okay, first you press this large button on your armrest and hold it in. Then you just push back against the seat or lean forward.
Man: I see, thank you.

Conversation Six
Woman: Is this the air control up here?
Man: I don't know. Excuse me ma'am, is this the air control?
Flight Attendant: Yes, it is. To open it, turn it clockwise, and to close it, turn it counterclockwise.

Exercise Two
Conversation One
Woman: Where is that light switch again?
Man: Um, let's see...push that thing up there next to the light.
Woman: I thought I had to push a button in the armrest here.
Man: No, I think it's up there, next to the light.

Conversation Two
Man: That's right, dear, just plug them in that little hole there, then push this button to adjust the volume, and—
Woman: Don't I turn this dial to adjust the volume?
Man: No, she said push the button for the volume! Turn the *dial* to change the channel!

Conversation Three
Man: I push this button with the light bulb to call the flight attendant, right?
Woman: No, not that button. Push the other button.
Man: What other button? I thought it was this button with the little light to call her...
Woman: No, no, push that button *next* to the light button to call her.

Conversation Four
Man: I can't get this food tray out!
Woman: Just pull the tray down, dear.
Man: No, no, you turn this thing here first and *then* pull the tray down.

Conversation Five
Man: This seat won't go back!
Woman: Just press that large button and—
Man: I *did* press it!
Woman: —and hold it in.
Man: What? No, you don't have to hold it in.

Conversation Six
Woman: Dear, could you turn that air control thing clockwise for me?
Man: You want it closed?
Woman: No, open.
Man: Well, to open it you turn it *counter*clockwise.
Woman: WILL YOU PLEASE TURN IT CLOCKWISE!

Conversation One
Woman: Could you do it today, honey? I just want to go straight home and lie down—my head is killing me.
Man: Well, okay. How do you use the machine?
Woman: Just put everything in and make sure the door is closed tight. Then pour one cup of soap in the little compartment in the top, and put in six quarters.

Man:	That's it?
Woman:	Oh yeah—set the temperature to hot. Just turn the dial.
Man:	Okay, no problem.
Woman:	And do you think you could pick up some groceries on the way home?

Conversation Two

Woman:	Excuse me, do you know what this is made of?
Salesman:	Yes, I do. The outside is sixty-five percent polyester and thirty-five percent cotton, and the lining is made of one hundred percent nylon. The filling is one hundred percent down.
Woman:	Does it have a hood?
Salesman:	Yes, it does. Just unzip the back of the collar and pull it out.

Conversation Three

Lou:	Excuse me, but I'm new here, and—
Nina:	No wonder I've never seen you before.
Lou:	Yeah, well, do you know how to—
Nina:	My name is Nina, by the way.
Lou:	Nina? Hi, I'm Lou, nice to meet you. Anyway, could you tell me how to use this? I mean, all these buttons...
Nina:	Oh, sure. Just put your page in here, face down, dial the number, and press this button here.
Lou:	I see, thanks.
Nina:	Anytime. Um, Lou, do you how to use the copier?

Conversation Four

Allison:	Shawn, can you get my ski jacket and wool scarf from the hall closet?
Shawn:	Sure...um, could you tell me what they look like? This closet is really full.
Allison:	Oh, well, the jacket is light blue and it has a white lining, and the scarf has blue and white stripes.
Shawn:	Oh, yeah, I got them...I think.
Allison:	And could you see if my sunglasses are in the inside pocket?
Shawn:	This jacket doesn't *have* an inside pocket, Allison.

Conversation Five

Woman:	I'm looking for something small and light.
Salesman:	Well, this one is very popular. As you can see, it has all the necessary attachments.
Woman:	I see...and how do you empty it?
Salesman:	Just press this button here, remove the front cover, and take out the bag. Then just slip a new bag in and close the cover. It's very easy.

UNIT 6   **Listening Task**   **Page 30**

Conversation One

Friend 1:	Okay if I smoke?
Friend 2:	Sure, go ahead.

Conversation Two

Son:	Is it okay if I use the new car tonight, Dad?
Dad:	I'd rather you didn't.

Conversation Three

Man:	Pardon me, I wonder if I could possibly use your phone?
Man:	I'm sorry, but it's out of order.

Conversation Four

Brother:	Hey, Sis! Do you mind if I borrow your laptop computer this weekend? I have a lot of homework to do.
Sister:	Sorry, I'm afraid not. I have to use it.

Conversation Five

Girl:	Can I go to a party Saturday night with Susan and Jenny?
Mom:	Well, okay. But don't be late.

Conversation Six

Friend 1:	Is it all right if I open this window?
Friend 2:	Of course.

Conversation Seven

Friend 1:	Mind if I turn off the TV? Nobody's watching it.
Friend 2:	No, go ahead.

Conversation Eight

Man:	Excuse me, Mr. Bellows. Would it be possible for me to take next Monday off? I have to take my sister home from the hospital.
Boss:	Uh huh—that'll be all right.

Conversation Nine

Man:	Hey, is it okay if I park here for a minute?
Man:	Sure.

Conversation Ten

Student:	Miss Riley, do you mind if I leave class early today? I have to meet a friend at the airport.
Teacher:	No, not at all.

UNIT 7   **Listening Task**   **Page 35**

[*Class bell rings.*]

Mrs. Fenway:	And don't forget to read Chapter Five and answer the questions on page ninety-nine! Oh, Jonathan, just a minute—I want to speak to you.
Jonathan:	Yes, Mrs. Fenway?
Mrs. Fenway:	Jonathan, why didn't you answer any questions on the homework?
Jonathan:	Oh, I'm sorry Mrs. Fenway, but I read the wrong chapter last night.
Mrs. Fenway:	Oh, I see. But why didn't you read the right chapter after you looked at the questions?
Jonathan:	Well, I had to do too much *other* homework last night.
Mrs. Fenway:	Now, Jonathan, You didn't have *that* much homework. You have to spend less time watching TV.
Jonathan:	Yes, Mrs. Fenway.
Mrs. Fenway:	And why were you late this morning?
Jonathan:	Oh, I had to walk to school because the school bus got a flat tire.
Mrs. Fenway:	A flat tire? Come on, Jonathan, no other students were late.
Jonathan:	Yeah, well, I couldn't walk fast because I have a sore foot.
Mrs. Fenway:	Oh, I'm sorry to hear that, Jonathan. Well, hurry to your next class or you'll be late.
Jonathan:	I will, Mrs. Fenway. See you tomorrow. [*Sound of running feet.*]
Mrs. Fenway:	Jonathan!
Jonathan:	Yes?
Mrs. Fenway:	Do not run in the hallway.
Jonathan:	Sorry.

Bob: Somebody will find us. I'm sure they're already looking for us...they'll find us, right John?

John: I don't know—they may never find us. I think we should build a raft and the four of us should sail out of here.

Sue: I agree with John—we have to get out of here ourselves.

Bob: I don't think so, Sue. I believe we're all safe here. There's plenty of food and water. In my opinion we should build a shelter and wait to be rescued. What do you think, Mary?

Mary: I don't agree with you, Bob. We can't wait forever. We have to do something—but I think that just one of us should try to get help, and the rest stay here.

John: Actually, I think that it's too dangerous out there for one person...

Bob: Right, John, I think so too. In my opinion we should all stick together.

Sue: That's true, but we can't just sit here!

Mary: I agree completely, Sue... Well then, I guess we should *all* go together, like John says...

Sue: Absolutely! Let's start working on a raft!

Conversation One

Man: I like the style, but I'm not sure about the fit. Do you have a bigger size?

Salesman: Just a moment. Ah, yes. Would you like to try these white ones?

Man: Sure, thanks. Oh yeah—these are much more comfortable. I'll take them.

Conversation Two

Man: You want the red one, huh?

Woman: Yeah. It's roomier than the blue one.

Man: Well, yes, but it's not as sporty as the blue one.

Woman: That's true, but I like the extra space—you know, for luggage...and for shopping...

Conversation Three

Lisa: They're cute, aren't they? Which one do you like, Janet?

Janet: The one on the right, I think. He's much more handsome.

Lisa: Do you think so? I like the other one. He looks more mature.

Janet: Look—they're coming this way, Lisa! What shall we do?

Conversation Four

Travel agent: How long do you have in mind?

Woman: I'm not sure—could you give me some idea of the prices?

Travel agent: Sure. Let's see, the Bali tour is ten days—that's $2500.

Woman: Do you have anything cheaper?

Travel agent: Our Phuket tour is about $2000, but it's not as long. It's eight days.

Conversation Five

Woman: Oh, yours is much better than mine!

Man: No, not at all—I think yours is as nice as mine.

Woman: No, no, no, not really. Mine is not nearly as nice as yours. I love yours.

Man: Oh, well, thank you. Here, please take it.

Woman: Oh no, I couldn't.

Man: No really, I insist.

Woman: Oh goodness...thank you.

Conversation One

Man: In my opinion, Paris is much more expensive than New York.

Woman: I couldn't agree more, but a nice apartment does cost a bit more in New York.

Man: That's true, but everything else, like food, entertainment, transportation—

Woman: Absolutely, especially if you drive here. Do you? Drive, I mean.

Man: As a matter of fact I do. I'm parked right over there. Would you care to go for a drive this afternoon?

Woman: That sounds lovely.

Conversation Two

Husband: I don't know, this is much more expensive than a three-speed bike. What do you think?

Wife: I think he'd enjoy the car more now, but actually, he'll use the bicycle a lot longer.

Husband: Yeah, I think so, too. We can get the bike *and* a few other presents with the extra money.

Wife: That's true. How about a new car for me?

Husband: Not *that* much extra, dear.

Conversation Three

Angela: Frankie, how did you *do* that?

Frankie: It wasn't my fault! A kid on a bike shot in front of my car and I went up the sidewalk and hit a telephone pole.

Angela: If you ask me, Dad is going to kill you!

Frankie: No he won't—I'm going to get it fixed like new.

Angela: How much do you think it's going to cost?

Frankie: I don't think it'll be more than five hundred dollars. By the way, Angela, could you lend me two hundred dollars?

Angela: Ha!

Frankie: Come on, *please*?

Conversation Four

Simon: But Mom, why can't I get a motorcycle? Lots of kids in high school have motorcycles—and they're cheaper than cars...

Mom: Simon, I don't care about other kids. Motorcycles are far more dangerous than cars, and you are still a new driver.

Simon: But motorcycles are more fun, and they're easier to park, and much better on gas.

Mom: What does your father think?

Simon: Well...he said no. But if you—

Mom: I agree with your father completely. The answer is no.

Conversation Five

Miss Lee: Joshua, I didn't see you at rehearsal yesterday. Where were you?

Joshua: I'm sorry, Miss Lee, but my brother needed help fixing his car. I had to go straight home yesterday.

Miss Lee: Well, don't miss it this afternoon, okay?

Joshua: I won't, I promise. But Miss Lee, I was wondering if I could hand in the final paper a few days late. I have to go Christmas shopping with my sister this weekend.

Miss Lee: Well, okay, but no later than Wednesday—and don't miss any more rehearsals. The school play is next week, Romeo.

Jenny: So, Elizabeth, what are you going to do for Sophie's graduation party?

Elizabeth: I don't know, Jenny—any ideas?

George: Why don't you rent a limousine to bring her to the party?

Elizabeth: A limo? I don't think so, George.

Jenny: You ought to rent one of those big wide-screen TVs and play music videos.

Elizabeth: Music videos—that sounds good, yeah.

George: And a band, Liz, you should get a live band! I know these guys—

Elizabeth: Um, that sounds interesting George, but that's a little expensive, and a lot of trouble.

George: Oh. Then, how about a disk jockey? I know this guy, and he's not expensive...

Elizabeth: Hmmm...yeah, that might be better. Music videos *inside* and a D.J. *outside*...let me think about it.

Jenny: Listen, why don't you have fireworks in the evening?

Elizabeth: Good idea, Jenny! Sophie loves fireworks! I hope it doesn't rain.

George: Maybe you'd better rent a big tent for the back yard.

Elizabeth: That *is* a good idea, George, but first I'll have to check the price, and the size of the tent.

Jenny: And if I were you, Elizabeth, I'd hire caterers to cook and serve the food.

Elizabeth: Caterers—yeah, that sounds like a good idea, too.

George: I know! How about Hawaiin belly-dancers serving the food, and...hey, where are you going?

Janet: Did you hear about the accident at this intersection last week?

Linda: Yeah, I saw it on TV. Pretty bad.

Janet: Have you ever had a bad car accident, Linda?

Linda: Yeah, a long time ago.

Janet: Really? What happened?

Linda: Well, I was driving with a friend in the city. We came to a red light and stopped in the right lane. There was a wall next to us, on the right. A really big truck pulled up next to us on the left. The light changed green, we started off, and the truck moved over to the right...and crushed my car against the wall. He just didn't see me!

Janet: Wow! Was anyone hurt?

Linda: No, we were really lucky—just scratched from broken glass. All the windows broke. When we stopped, the wall was on the right and the truck was on the left, and we couldn't get out of the doors! So we had to climb out through the windshield.

Janet: Gee, you *were* lucky—you could've been killed!

Linda: Yeah. Anyway, since then I've always been real careful of trucks, like that one up there on the left.

Janet: And I bet you're not crazy about driving next to walls, like this one on the right.

Linda: Oh, red light. [*Sound of truck.*]

Janet and Linda: Uh-oh...

[*Telephone rings.*]

Mia: Hello?

Zachary: Hello, Mia? This is Zachary.

Mia: Oh, hi, Zachary, what's up?

Zachary: Oh, nothing much. Are you busy this weekend?

Mia: Well, a little. Why?

Zachary: Would you like to see a movie Friday night?

Mia: I'd love to, Zachary, but I'm going to watch TV at Yuriko's house Friday night.

Zachary: Oh, I see, okay. Well how about going swimming Saturday afternoon?

Mia: I'm sorry, but I have a French class Saturday afternoon.

Zachary: And I guess you're busy Saturday night, too, right? I mean, do you feel like going bowling Saturday night?

Mia: That sounds great, Zachary, but I'm going to a birthday party for a girl in my French class. Sorry.

Zachary: Sunday night, Mia! Dinner! How about having dinner Sunday night? Or are you—

Mia: Sure, that's a great idea.

Zachary: What?

Mia: I said that's a great idea.

Zachary: Oh. Really?

Mia: Really. I'd love to.

Zachary: *Oh, no...*

Mia: What's the matter?

Zachary: Sunday night I have to pick up a friend at the airport...

Mia: Oh, well, maybe another time, then.

Jack: So tell me, Loni, is Harry ready for his trip?

Loni: Yeah, he finished packing this evening.

Jack: Where is he now?

Loni: Out with some friends.

Jack: Well, we have to go to the airport at six in the morning, so— Hey, what's the matter?

Loni: Jack, I'm a little nervous about Harry's trip to Japan—I mean, Japan is so far away.

Jack: Come on, honey, he's twenty-two years old, he's got a great job, and he speaks a little Japanese. I'm sure he's going to have a great time.

Loni: But we won't see him for *one year!*

Jack: Don't worry. The time will probably pass very quickly.

Loni: But what if he stays there? He might meet a girl and have a family over there!

Jack: So what's wrong with that? He'll keep in touch.

Loni: I guess so, but maybe he'll never come back!

Jack: Then we can visit him in Japan, okay?

Loni: Well, okay. Maybe we should start learning Japanese, huh?

Jack: Now that's a good idea. *Arigato.*

Loni: Harry got two? Harry got two what?

Jack: No, no—I said "*Arigato.*" That's Japanese for "Thank you." Harry taught me a few words.

Conversation One

Man: So, how do you like it?

Woman: Well, it's okay, but... Have you ever been caught in a storm?

Man: No, not really. A little rain, maybe...

Woman: Well, I think there's going to be a storm.

Man: Nah, it may rain a *little*, but I'm sure that there won't be a storm. [*Sound of thunder, followed by heavy rainfall.*]

Woman: WE ARE GOING TO DROWN! WE ARE DEFINITELY GOING TO DROWN!

Man: MAYBE WE'D BETTER ROW TO SHORE...

Conversation Two

George: Good morning, Jenny. Hey, you don't look so good. What's the matter?

Jenny: Oh, I feel awful! I have a terrible headache, and I'm so tired...

George: Why don't you go home early? I'm sure the boss will understand.

Jenny: Yeah, I know, but my desk will probably fill up with work while I'm out.

George: If I were you, I'd forget about work. You ought to take the day off and—hey! Would you like to go hiking this weekend? We could—

Jenny: George, please, you've got to be kidding! Oh, my head...

Conversation Three

Woman: I think I'd better—

Man: Dear, let me do this, okay?

Woman: But don't you think I should turn the water off first?

Man: I've fixed drains a dozen times before. Could you hand me that wrench?

Woman: Okay, but it might leak.

Man: It'll be okay, could you just—[*Sound of gushing water*]—could you just turn off the water, please?

Conversation Four

Woman: Let's do something different this weekend. We could go out. How about going to the beach?

Man: It's going to rain.

Woman: Oh, well, would you like to go rollerblading?

Man: Nah, I've never gone rollerblading before—I don't know how.

Woman: Okay, then, do you feel like going to the movies?

Man: Nah. Hey, we haven't been to the video store in a while. Let's rent a few movies.

Woman: Sure, that would be real different.

Conversation Five

Man: See? It's not so bad, right?

Woman: Why don't we set up the tent?

Man: Come on, this will be great!

Woman: I think we'll be eaten alive by mosquitoes.

Man: I've never had a problem with mosquitoes. [*Sounds of coyote and bear in distance.*] Um, you're right. I think we'd better sleep in the car. Could you give me the keys?

Woman: The keys? I don't have the keys! I thought *you* had the keys!

GRAMMAR SUMMARIES

Unit 1   Asking for Information

I'd like some information about	the buses. the bus to Boston.	Sure. How can I help you? Yes?

Do you know Could you tell me	what time it leaves? how long it takes? how much it costs? if you have an express bus? the best time to leave?	It leaves at 7:55 in the morning. It takes one and a half hours. One way is $20, and round trip is $35. Yes, we do. The best time to leave is early morning.

Unit 2   Describing Things

What does it look like? Could you tell me what it looks like? Do you know what it looks like?

It's	small long	and	square. flat.
	black dark blue	and it has	stripes. polka dots.
It has	a zipper. buttons.		

What is it made of? Could you tell me what it's made of? Do you know what it's made of?

It's made of	leather. wood. cotton. plastic and metal.

Unit 3   Making Requests

Can you Could you	close the door? lend me your pen?		
Do you think you could Could you possibly	meet me after school? pick me up tomorrow?		
Would it be possible for you to I was wondering if you could possibly		help me move tomorrow? take me to the airport later?	
Would you mind	closing the door? turning down the volume?		

(Yes) Sure. Of course. I'd be glad to. No problem.	*(No)* I'm sorry, but I wish I could, but I'd like to, but I'm afraid I can't.	I'm very busy. I have to work.
Not at all. No, not at all.		

Unit 4   Giving Instructions

How can I How do you Could you tell me how to	buy a parking receipt from this machine?

First, put in the money for the amount of time you want. Then, push this green button. After that, take your receipt from the machine.

GRAMMAR SUMMARIES *(continued)*

Unit 6   Asking for Permission

				(Yes)	(No)	
Okay if I	sit down?			Sure.	I'd like to, but	it doesn't work.
Can I	close the door?			Sure, go ahead.	I'm sorry, but	I have to use it.
Could I	borrow your pen?			Of course.	Sorry, but I'm afraid that	
Is it okay if I	use your phone?					
Is it all right if I	wear your jacket?					
I wonder if I could		borrow your camera?				
Would it be possible for me to		use your car?				
Mind if I	sit down?			Not at all.		
Do you mind if I	use your phone?			No, go ahead.		
				No, please do.		

Unit 7   Making Excuses and Giving Reasons

Did you	fix the car?	I'm sorry.	I couldn't find the keys.
Why didn't you	clean the garage?	Sorry, but	I had to do a lot of homework.
			I didn't have time.
			I forgot.

Unit 8   Giving Opinions

I think (that)	smoking cigarettes should not be allowed in public places.
I believe (that)	
In my opinion,	
I don't think (that) smoking cigarettes should be allowed in public places.	

(Agree)	(Disagree)	
I think so, too.	I don't think so.	Smokers have rights, too.
That's true.	That's true, but...	
I agree with you.	I disagree.	
I don't think so either.	I don't agree with you.	

Unit 9   Comparing Things

The Volkswagon	is smaller than	the Cadillac.
	is more economical than	
	isn't as comfortable as	

Is the Volkswagon	easier to park than	the Cadillac?	Yes, it is.
	more popular than		I'm not sure.
	as roomy as		No, it isn't.

Which is	faster,	the Volkswagon or the Cadillac?	The Cadillac (is).
	more expensive,		

Unit 11 Giving Advice and Making Suggestions

What's	wrong? the matter?		I have a toothache. I lost my credit card.

You should You ought to You'd better Why don't you If I were you, I'd	go to the dentist. call the credit card company.	Yes, Yeah, Right,	I'm going to. that's a good idea. I think I will. maybe I will. I guess I should.

Unit 12 Talking About Experiences

Have you ever	gone surfing? ridden a camel? been to Hawaii?	Yes, I have. No, I haven't.

When Where Who	did you	go? ride one? go with?	I went last summer. I rode one in Egypt. I went with my friends.

Unit 13 Inviting

Would you like to	go to the movies tonight?
How about Do you feel like	going to the beach tomorrow?

(Accept) I'd love to. That sounds great. That's a great idea.	(Refuse) I'd love to, but That sounds great, but I'm sorry, but	I have to study for a test.

Unit 14 Making Predictions

I'm sure they'll They're definitely going to	win the game on Sunday. come tonight.
They'll They're going to	call us later. be late tomorrow.
I think they'll They'll probably	
Maybe they'll They could They might	